YOU ARE YOUR BUSINESS

How to be a great businessman starting from zero

Frank Norving

Copyright © 2019 Frank Norving

All rights reserved.

ISBN: 9781688222533

Contents

INTRODUCTION 1

CHAPTER ONE 5

THE POWER OF SELF-BELIEF 5

    How to build self-belief 8

    Finding the Balance: Self-Belief and Listening to Others 12

CHAPTER TWO 15

LISTENING: THE SECRET THAT ALL SUCCESSFUL BUSINESS LEADERS KNOW 15

    The benefits of listening 20

    Do you hear or do you listen? 23

CHAPTER 3 26

PAST DEFEATS OR STEPPING STONE 26

    Learning how to use defeat to your advantage 29

    You don't have to be defeated, learn from others. 33

CHAPTER FOUR 37

WHY YOU NEED TO BE CURIOUS AS A LEADER 37

    How to develop curiosity 41

    How to inspire curiosity in others as a leader 44

CHAPTER FIVE 49

LEARNING TO LOOK FOR THE MOST IMPORTANT ELEMENT/QUESTION 49

    If you are critical, be constructive 54

Ways to inspire a culture of critical observation in the workplace 55

CHAPTER SIX 59

USE SUCCESS TO FIND SUCCESS 59

CHAPTER SEVEN 65

CREATE AND BE IMAGINATIVE 65

How to be creative as a leader 69

How to promote creativity in the workplace? 73

CHAPTER EIGHT 77

BUILD A TEAM THAT UNDERSTANDS YOU 77

What is a team? 77

The Advantages of a strong team 80

Qualities to look out for in a team that understands you 83

How to be a team player as a leader 86

CHAPTER 9 89

GRATITUDE, A LEADER'S BEST FRIEND 89

How can you appreciate your team in the workplace? 92

How to promote the appreciation culture in your workplace 94

CHAPTER TEN 99

HOW TO TREAT TEAM MEMBERS 99

Why you should keep your team-members happy 101

    How to treat team-members well.......................... 104

    Dealing with difficult members of the team.......... 110

CHAPTER ELEVEN 119

LIVE IN THE PRESENT 119

    Moving beyond the past... 121

    How to use the experiences of the past 122

    Success is a combination of failure and success ... 124

CHAPTER 12.. 129

MONEY IS A BONUS, NOT THE TARGET 129

CHAPTER THIRTEEN 137

INTEGRITY AND HONESTY AS ESSENTIAL COMMODITIES IN THE BUSINESS SPACE................... 137

    Why leaders need honesty and integrity............... 138

    Stories of trust gone sour 140

    How to inspire honesty in the workplace 143

CONCLUSION.. 147

INTRODUCTION

The **Fortune 500** is one of the world's most exclusive list. Every entry on the list represents a story of great sacrifices and unparalleled excellence. Each entry tells a story of excellence and perfection mixed with the best of creative solutions that the world currently possesses. Each company listed in the *Fortune* 500 tells a tale of triumph over mitigating factors. The list represents the world's version of current business Olympians.

Now, each day, new businesses spring up along the world. Every one of them starts up in the hope of making it to the top one day. Consciously or subconsciously, the ultimate target for each of these businesses is the *Fortune 500*. Getting featured among even the top one million companies in the world is no mean feat however. It is a task that seems to be beyond most seasoned people in business. Managing even to scrape any form of profit from their enterprises is a big ask for most business owners and entrepreneur. The result is that less than 10% of businesses remain viable a decade after their formation.

What drives these businesses into extinction and loss? Why do more people fail than succeed in business? Why has your business stagnated? Why can you not seem to even break?

These are questions that must be answered before you can move into even the top lists of your country. The answers to these questions will help you understand what the companies at the top end of the *Fortune 500* do regularly. Yearly, thousands of books are written to define the answers. Prospective entrepreneurs gobble them up and try to replicate the methods without much success.

Admittedly, the problem cannot be with the people trying to replicate all the rules of leveraging or diversification. Surely, if the methods were correct, then we should have seen more success, right? Well, it turns out that the methods, while being practical, are not based in the right direction. The *correct* methods are focused on the wrong problem.

Dear reader, I tell you now that your business is not the problem; the market demand for your products is not the problem. You are the problem! Allow that to sink in. I know it sounds harsh, but that is the truth. Your business is stagnating because you have not fixed **you.**

Why do I say this? Most businesses today are so focused on the revenue indices that they miss out the reason why clients come to them. They leave out that personal touch and try to get their business figures and revenue stats to speak for them. A cursory look at most business revealed something to me. Most businesses are failing because they have a problem in producing at least one of the following areas;

- A seamless client relationship
- Smart product development and management
- A healthy working environment

Client relationship determines who is going to buy your products. Even more importantly, it determines if a client is going to come back to you when they need that same service again. The more clients who return to you, the more revenue you generate. To keep these clients hooked to your brand, you need a product that continues to sell itself to them. Now, the problem is that every other competitor out there has the same or a similar product. So, you need to do one of two things;

- Be creative enough to produce a unique service or product
- Offer your product in a different way

This is where a healthy working environment comes to play. To achieve client satisfaction and engender innovative solutions, there is a need to produce a healthy team spirit among your staff.

These are the differences that top businesses employ to beat loss and increase the chances of success. Learning to run a business is cool, but until you learn to direct and run the people who make up your business well, you will never make it out of the woods. That is why I have written this book as a different offering to every other one on the market. It teaches you business leadership in a very different way to what you are used to.

By applying the principles within the book, you can learn to grow your business without hassles. By learning to lead your business, you can move from zero to hero.

Good luck as you make the move to become successful in business!

CHAPTER ONE

THE POWER OF SELF-BELIEF

"Once we believe in ourselves, we can risk curiosity, wonder, spontaneous delight, or any experience that reveals the human spirit."

- EE Cummings.

If you happen to run into some of the greatest leaders who ever lived, you will discover that there is one common trait they have other than their pedigrees, skills, talents, and intelligence. These individuals, either in medieval or modern times, all possessed insanely high amounts of self-belief and confidence.

If you are patient enough to study their lives, you will find out that they are very much like you. Some of them started from humble backgrounds, many of them faced difficulties which threatened to tear them down, wear them out and steal from them the most essential ingredients they needed for success, happiness, and fulfillment. They succeeded because they were stronger than their circumstances. They succeeded because nothing could steal the thunder from their self-belief. So, what is self-belief?

Self-belief is that feeling of confidence, and self-assurance in yourself, your abilities and your capabilities. It is the ability to lay plans for tomorrow even on the bleakest of days. Interestingly, it is no cliché that all humans were indeed born equal, irrespective of their nationality, sexuality, and personality.

As infants, when we could barely relate with the meaning of class, race, pedigree, failure, success, and the other definitions that define human existence, everyone is extremely confident (if confidence is sufficient enough as a term to describe the state). We are fearless enough to stick our fingers in the fire, and face what adults run away from.

Sadly, as we grow up, we encounter denials, disappointments, delays, and different events that dampen our spirits, quench the fire that burns within and dilutes our self-belief. Self-belief, more important than skills, talents, or gifts, is one of the most straightforward traits to lose. However, it is essential to know that belief can turn a mountain into a molehill or give a dog the strength of a lion.

Our different experiences as we grow up, give us different levels of belief, and that comes to play in adult life. If you grow up in an environment that builds your confidence, you will most likely grow up to live a life that distinguishes you from your contemporaries as an optimistic, upbeat, and never-say-never individual. However, if you grow up in an environment that dampens your zest, zeal, and self-belief, you may also grow up to be pessimistic, demoralized, and eventually a failure at leading people.

Now, the problem with self-belief is that, as you think, dear reader, so will you be. The power resides in you; the power resides in your mind. The power to become a leader of worth lies in the unwavering strength of self-belief. Success or failure, victory or defeat, lies in the ability of an individual to believe in their skills, and channel that belief into productive ends.

It is true that whatever the mind dares to conceive, and the individual dares to believe, the individual will undoubtedly achieve. Without self-belief, what is left for the individual is nothing other than self-doubt.

As EE Cummings said, "once we activate within, the power of self-belief in our minds it opens a new vista of curiosity, wonder and spontaneous delight that self –doubt has kept veiled from us for a long time." There is so much priceless value in believing in oneself. The tree that stands strong and firm today was a seed that believed in itself irrespective of the howling winds, the raging storms, and unfavorable conditions.

The lion that walks in the jungle today was a cub that believed that he could be anything with time, patience, and belief. Most importantly, that leader you admire today was once a follower who studied, understood, and applied the power of self-belief. Are you ready to take the journey into self-belief?

How to build self-belief
Let me open this with a quote from foremost American novelist, Mark Twain. He said, "Twenty years from now you will be more disappointed by the things you didn't do than by the ones you did do. So, throw off the bowlines. Sail away from the safe harbor. Catch the trade winds in your sail. Explore. Dream. Discover."

The life of an individual who is filled with self-doubt is characterized by unfulfilled dreams, uncoordinated thoughts, unvisited destinations, and undecided decisions, and much more. Borrowing the words of Mark Twain, if one were to advance twenty years in the life of an indecisive and pessimistic individual, the end would be filled with regret for things that haven't been done.

There are many steps to take that can help move a businessperson from zero to hero; these time-tested principles and practices can take an individual from the nadir to the zenith of their life. Let us consider a few in this part of the book.

- **Utilize the power of visualization**: visualization is the act or technique of imagining yourself a success already. It is almost like daydreaming about the future, with one notable exception; you are a qualified success in the daydream. Having something like that to look forward to can give you the required impetus to get to where you want to be. That is how visualization works. Self-doubt is a product of poor perception of yourself. But by utilizing the power of visualization, you can create a new reality for yourself.

- **Do something new for a change**: if you want to build your self-belief, you have to learn to do new things for a change. There is a trait common in individuals who battle with self-doubt. It is the fact that they are comfortable with the status quo; they are complacent while doing the same thing all year long. They are afraid to do something new, and try a different path. They are frozen by the fear of change, and until this cycle is broken, they will remain stuck in old ways. Each new experience imbues you with confidence and belief in yourself. As you face your fears heads on, you will discover that all the fears were unfounded.

- **Utilize the power of affirmation**: it is easier to cross from self-doubt to self- belief by understanding and utilizing the power of affirmation. Affirmations involve saying or writing positive and uplifting statements that are in line with the image we want of ourselves.

Affirmations are as powerful as visualization, and when both are combined, they set in motion a form of 're-programming' for your mind. No statement is as profound and credible like the those we say aloud to ourselves. Nikki Carnevale summed it up when she said 'Affirmations are a powerful tool to install desired beliefs about yourself deliberately." What more conviction do you need to get started on them already?

- **Learn to silence that inner voice:** You may have begun the journey to self-belief. You may have had a winning streak after visualizing, affirming and succeeding in a few things until you suddenly hit a bend in the road. Don't be surprised that your most prominent critic will be you. Many people hit a temporary slump, and turn against themselves, putting themselves down at every opportunity. They find an inner voice that is so quick to berate and belittle their efforts and results, respectively.

You have to learn to silence that voice, quickly and as often as it pops up. If you can question that inner voice and find the lessons that need to be learned, then you should file the rest away. They are unnecessary and unhealthy for you. Much more than shutting out the inner critic, you must also learn to congratulate and commend yourself as much as you condemn yourself. This is very vital for building self-belief.

- **Set SMART goals**: most times, people set themselves up for failure and consequently, when they fail, self-doubt arises. Failing at unattainable goals that you set always leads to a drop in confidence. So, why not set SPECIFIC, MEASURABLE, ACHIEVABLE, AND REALISTIC goals that can be achieved in the right TIMEFRAME? Set goals that pass these five criteria instead of just wiring out goals that you have a limited chance of achieving.

- **Never compare yourself with someone else**: To build your self-esteem, learn to stop the habit of comparison and competition. It is good to chart your progress and compare it with your peers, but it is unhealthy for you to allow that to attain negative dimensions. The problem with most individuals in leadership posts is that they tend to compare themselves with others. They keep up with the Jones's, or measure themselves or their performances against other people unnecessarily. The effect of this is that the individual never measures up, never feels satisfied. Eventually, they end up losing all form of confidence and belief in their abilities. It is these folks Marilyn Monroe was referring to when she said "wanting to be someone else is a waste of the person you are."

Finding the Balance: Self-Belief and Listening to Others

You may have moved from self-doubt to self-belief. You may have moved from the streets of pessimism to the avenue of optimism and self-assurance. Everything seems perfect now, but there is something else, something seems to be missing.

Self-belief can be a blessing or a curse, and it all depends on the individual. There is a very thin line between self-belief and pure, blatant overconfidence and arrogance.

Taken too far in a negative sense, it can warp you into thinking your voice is the only one that matters. That is just untrue. Therefore, you need to strike a balance between listening to people and listening to yourself.

Tilting too much to one side has its effect. Listening to people's opinion constantly and making it always influence your decision will make you 'less of yourself.' While listening only to yourself will lead you to make avoidable but costly mistakes, and eventually alienate you from friends, associates, and mentors.

The objective of this book is not to make you self-opinionated, overconfident, and full of yourself. The objective of this book is to allow you to find a healthy balance. The purpose is to help you become a great leader, and not some conceited, self-interested

As a wise head once said, 'Balance is the rule of life.' As a person in business, you will be surrounded by different individuals regardless of the stage you are in. These individuals may include business partners, business analysts, investors, colleagues, subordinates, and in some cases, the competition.

Some of the conversations may be valuable, and others may be valueless. Some might be filled with wisdom, and others may be filled with gibberish. These conversations you will have may be constructive or destructive, and they will certainly affect your confidence, positively or negatively.

Some might inspire a quick reaction or require a well-thought-out response from you, but the most important thing to do is to learn from the words of Aristotle when he said, "...gentleness is the ability to bear reproaches and slights with moderation and not to embark on revenge quickly and not to be easily provoked to anger, but to be free from bitterness and contentiousness, having tranquility and stability in the spirit."

In conclusion, you cannot be a leader if you do not possess a great deal of self-belief in your abilities to get things done. It is an absolute prerequisite for leading people.

CHAPTER TWO

LISTENING: THE SECRET THAT ALL SUCCESSFUL BUSINESS LEADERS KNOW

"The more you talk about them, the more important they will feel. The more you listen to them, the more important you will make them feel."

— *Roy T. Bennett*

You might be good at making grandiloquent speeches. You might be excellent in making a sales pitch. You might be magnificent in arousing emotion in people whenever you speak. However, there is something much more important in business and life than a persuasive tongue and oratory prowess.

The overwhelming importance of listening cannot be overemphasized. Nature understands this so much so that every individual is created with a single mouth and double ears showing that speaking may be important and might even come first, but listening is more vital, and it should be done more often than speaking.

Come to think of it, from when we were barely toddlers; we have always been attracted to those who listened to us. We spent more time with those we were most comfortable with. As time progressed, we began to form alliances and associations with "friends," the ones that were patient enough to listen to us in spite of their competing and conflicting schedules.

Interestingly, we named a special person, our best friend, because they were the ones willing to give up everything to attend to us every time. They might not be good at talking; they might not be best at playing. But they certainly were the best at listening. As we evolved to become adults, we developed a certain attraction for other individuals too, subordinates or maybe our mentees. We began to develop affinity and show preferential treatments to those who 'listened more to us.

That's exactly the way everyone loves those who listen to us. Those who talk less and listen more pick up more than just words even. They can discern better and decode body language. Poker is a game that emphasizes this; keeping a straight face while being able to listen to little details can make all the difference in the game. That's the same way it works in the business and leadership worlds too. Listen to people more; they will say more. Listen to people, and you will hear beyond their words.

Dear reader, you will discover from all this unconscious journey which the following lines has just brought to your consciousness, that there is so much power in listening. There is just too much unlimited, untapped, and unexplored power in listening to others.

Ralph G. Nichols made an amazing discovery, and he expressed it in words when he said this about human needs, "The most basic of all human needs is the need to understand and be understood. The best way to understand people is to listen to them." Do you want your business to succeed? Listen to the needs of the market. Do you want people to regard your words with reverence? Listen to theirs with rapt attention.

Leaders from time immemorial and in the present time have also made this discovery about listening and have put it into practice. It has continued to produce great results and massive rewards. Proactive leaders in government and business have discovered that although people might like you for what you say, they will love you, follow you and follow your vision if you listen to them more. Listening is an innate need in humans; it is a fundamental need. It is a need every upcoming leader in business must endeavor to fill.

Very few people are more qualified to talk about the immense power of listening than the late American statesman, philanthropist, consultant, financer, stock investor and businessman, Bernard Baruch, who stated that "Most of the successful people I've known are the ones who do more listening than talking." After working with two American presidents, and being a leader for a large part of his life, it can be assumed that he knows what he is saying.

The best part is that listening is a trait of leadership which can be developed with time and practice no matter how 'restless' you may be or how 'un-quiet' people describe you as. Roy Bennet reiterates how essential listening is when he said "The more you talk about people, the more important they feel, but if you try letting them talk and you listen, you just gave them the power; the power to feel important and you will be glad you did because everyone loves to be in charge."

To be fairly candid, listening seems harder than talking. The natural inclination is to want to force your truth and opinion down the throat of other people, but that never turns out well most times. Instead, you can learn more and have less reason to force people to do things by listening to them and make them feel in charge.

Listening is important in business leadership for a lot of reasons. It fosters team spirit. It makes the leader learn more. It makes the followers learn from the leader, and it allows for peace and co-existence in any community.

One of the most important things leaders always look forward to is the result. Leaders always want goals to be reached, targets to be met, and results delivered. The consciousness of these factors will make a leader inspire, inform, and communicate regularly and better with their staff or and associates. While speaking, instructing, directing, and giving orders might seem to be actions that work, listening in the right way is often ignored.

There are numerous possibilities in listening that leaders need to look into and learn from, to take their business or organization to the next level. It is possible to fall into the error of hearing and not listening. It is possible to make the mistake of listening and not applying. As leaders, it is possible to flip the script and pay attention to our followers because it is only then that we can enjoy the possibilities that abound in listening.

Listening has a whole lot of possibilities it can bring to life, but let us check out a few of the more convincing ones.

The benefits of listening

"Listening to others' viewpoints may reveal the one thing needed to complete your goals."

– D. Ridgley

- **Listening creates an environment of trust**: nothing is as disheartening as working in an atmosphere where trust is lost. Unfortunately, this is what is obtainable in most work environments. Successful business leaders know that when they listen to their associates, and employees, they can inspire more commitment from them because they feel they are being trusted, and their opinions count. This is what listening does. When you listen, as an emerging business leader, your employees know that you don't see them as mere tools or steps to get to the next destination. You will discover that they will do more than is expected of them because they feel like part of a team.
- **Listening allows you to learn**: there is no gainsaying that listening is very vital when it comes to learning. It worked in school; it worked when you learned a new skill or

craft. It worked when you made that profitable investment choice. It is only egocentric or careless individuals that ignore the role listening plays in daily life.

Do you want to learn from your subordinates? Listen! Do you want to learn from your contemporaries? Listen! Do you want to learn from your superiors? Master the art of listening. What you know and all you know can be exhausting and can also be exhausted, but what you need to know from listening to others is inexhaustible. Great leaders understand this so much, which is why they have mastered the act of listening intently and intensely. They have learned that the best of lessons is often found after listening to the people they surround themselves with.

- **Listening allows you to make friends**: we all want to be a boss; we all seek to be a leader. We all want to be the head, but have we tried being a friend? Bosses are respected. Rulers are feared. The heads of organizations or families are honored, but friends are the most reliable and dependable of them all. To truly inspire the kind of commitment that can catapult you into the stratosphere, you need to learn to become friends with the people you want to lead. Understandably, the workplace requires more workers. It is not debatable that leaders need committed followers, but it is also important to note that even businesses need friends and bosses needs allies.

One of the possibilities that listening affords us is the fact that the more you listen to people, the more they see you as a friend. Followers may do as they are told; workers may work till the close of work, but only friends will go the extra mile. This is the importance of friendship. Businesses that survive and thrive are those built by individuals willing to go the extra mile. Most times, these people are workers who have become friends or followers who have become pals. All the time, this transition is inspired by listening.

- **Listening makes you influential**. Have you ever heard that "your net worth is equal to your network?" What this means is that as a business person, your affluence is proportional to your influence. It is almost impossible to find an affluent individual who isn't influential. It is also impossible to find an influential person who isn't a listener. Businesses thrive on influence. Someone once said, "you can't be rich until you learn how to reach (people)." Reaching doesn't mean you do all the talking. Sometimes, it needs you to listen to your staff, the market, and the competition.

Do you hear or do you listen?

"There's a lot of difference between listening and hearing."

— *G. K. Chesterton*

The art of listening is one of the most misunderstood concepts in the world. Listening is much more than staying mute. Listening is an active action of staying quiet, avoiding judgments and receiving information without bias.

There have been thousands of teachings, and millions of articles detailing the difference between listening and hearing, and just like G.K Chesterton said, "there is indeed a huge difference between listening and hearing.

The mistake most people make is that they hear and do not listen. To hear means to pretend to listen but with the intent to reply. So, you will find out that most people spend so much time interrupting the other person mid-sentence. People who hear and but do not listen will display several other disruptive physical reactions and eventually, fail to grasp the crux of the matter being discussed.

Interestingly this is the challenge with a whole lot of people. Stephen Covey once said, "Most people do not listen with the intent to understand; they listen with the intent to reply." The consequence of engaging in this form of "listening" is that trust is lost, time is wasted, and vital lessons are missed.

It may sound like a cliché but "The word listen contains the same letters as the word silent, and if your definition of listening does not involve being silent by shutting your mouth and being silent internally by quietening your mind, then all you are doing is mere hearing.

The worst part, if you only hear, is that people always know when you are not listening. People see through the smokescreen and as Raquel Welch said 'you cannot fake listening, it shows. When you do not listen, you miss all the important facts. Building a business from "nowhere" to "now here" requires listening. Building a business from zero to hero status requires "paying attention." Pay attention to research and trends. Pay attention to understand customer psychology. Pay attention to study your associates or your staff.

Karl Menninger said, "listening is a magnetic force" which means if you listen to others, others will listen to you, but if you pretend to listen to others, they will pretend to listen to you. It is as simple as that. If you want to master the art of listening, try this sequence as stated by one wise head; "Listen thrice. Think twice. Speak once."

Listen to everyone and everything around you. It will help you miss the potholes on the road. It will give people the status they require and deserve to work with your vision. It will help you conclude negotiations faster and smoother.

CHAPTER 3

PAST DEFEATS OR STEPPING STONE

"The ability to bounce back after a setback is the most critical trait any entrepreneurial venture can possess."

- Richard Branson

In case you are still in doubts, let me state it loud and clear. You will fail before you succeed. There will be major setbacks in your journey towards success. You have two choices then; expect the defeats and ride them when they come, or dread them and allow them to ride you when they happen.

Nothing comes with the territory in business as much as defeats, delays, and failures. If you have tried anything worthwhile ever, you would have noticed that failures characterize this journey more than success. The catch is that the success at the end transcends all the failures put together.

If you are a keen observer, you will notice that the "concept" of failure is one that trails every successful venture. Have you ever considered the number of times a growing toddler falls over when trying to walk? Have you ever wondered why every seed planted in the soil usually dies before it sprouts? Why do most businesses fail at least ten times in the first five years of their inception?

Failures, defeats, setbacks, or hindrances have trailed the lives of the successful and the unsuccessful. What you call failure, has shaped the lives of many. It has been responsible for the success of some, and the demise of others.

We all know these about failure, but most people never ask why the little child did not stop trying after falling for the umpteenth time. Why didn't the seed stop growing after it died?

Dear reader, it is vital to know that there is no such thing as defeat. This assertion may sound irrational and unbelievable. But there is every ounce of truth to it.

On your journey to business success, will you lose money? Will you lose friends? Will you miss opportunities and chances? And sometimes, will you lose hope? The answer to these questions is a resounding "yes." You will lose all these many times over.

But are these moments of darkness, bleakness, and weakness, moments of defeats? Well, the answer is up to you. In this chapter of this mind-altering book, I will show you how what you call failure can be the best moment of your business, existence, and your life.

Like the little child that gets up after falling after ever attempt at walking, like an individual who gets up every time they graze their knee while trying to ride a bicycle, the ability to bounce back after every fall and after every setback is an essential trait every business person needs to master.

Richard Branson, a serial entrepreneur and CEO of the world-renowned brand, The Virgin Group, has probably experienced more failures than you. Richard Branson has a word to say about defeats and setbacks. While acknowledging that defeats are commonplace in business while acknowledging that there are many traits a business person needs to possess, but he said "The ability to bounce back after a setback is the most critical trait an entrepreneurial venture can possess."

It is a trait needed for survival; your business future is determined to a larger extent by how you handle failure than by how you grow your success. There are no good or bad situations; there are just good or bad perceptions. It is your perception and reaction to these "unfavorable" situations in your life that will make what seems like a setback to become a springboard for you.

Setbacks are just learning experiences designed to help you understand the process of success better. Think of them as a screening exercise for those who are not good or strong enough to succeed. They help weed those kinds of people out and narrow the pool of those that will succeed.

How can you ensure that you do not get weeded out?

Learning how to use defeat to your advantage

> *"Remember that setbacks are only challenges in disguise. Look at them as lessons don't waste time beating yourself up. Just get back on track and focus on what you want. It's up to you, and you will do it!"*
>
> *– Jorge Cruise*

Read the quote above again. Done? Now, go back and reread it. Let the message sink in. The message it bears is what this section is all about.

Only a fool will not say it as it is. Defeats are painful, failure is dreadful, and disappointments are stressful. They often come unplanned; they often spring up when you are least prepared. And they often do more harm than good.

Have you ever thought about the state of Thomas Edison's mind while he ran thousands of unsuccessful experiments to perfect the light bulb? Do you ever wonder what crossed Abraham Lincoln's mind as he kept losing election after election? Have you ever wondered if British writer and bestselling author of the Harry Potter series, J.K Rowling, shed tears and felt depressed when she was turned down by several publishers? When he was fired from a company he started in his father's garage, do you ever imagine if Steve Jobs threw his hands in the air in despair and walked away swearing never to try again?

Almost all the biggest businesses today started from a place of failure and had to grasp with a lot of defeats and failure. Most of these successful individuals did have some immediate negative reactions to moments of failure, defeats, disappointments, and setbacks. However, the reason why you are reading about them now is that they didn't stop to lick their wounds. They didn't give up; they didn't listen to the "no" from outside neither did they listen to the "you're not good enough" from within. The difference between these individuals and the ones you may never read about or hear about is the simple fact that these individuals understood and applied one of the most important lessons of success and learned to use their defeats to your advantage.

Consider the story of Steve Jobs who was sent out of *Apple*: a company he built from scratch to rise from less than a thousand bucks to a company that was worth many millions in dollars. Just like the average individual, this single act was enough to make him give up and embrace defeat. But what Steve did instead will blow your mind but most importantly, will make you know what to do when faced with defeat rather than feeling defeated.

Steve Jobs started two more companies, learning from the experience of the past, and combining it with the steely resilience he had developed in the present. The new companies, *NeXT* and *Pixar*, became global brands only a few years after Jobs had been shooed out of *Apple*. Less than a decade later, he was called back to join (save) *Apple*, a company he then built to become one of the most valuable companies in the world. Talk about a bounce-back. Talk about making a feat out of defeat. Talk about the quintessential example of using failure to your advantage.

Jorge Cruise has this to say to you; "Remember that setbacks are only challenges in disguise. Look at them as lessons and don't waste time beating yourself up. Just get back on track and focus on what you want. It's up to you, and you will do it!"

Steven Spielberg is a legend in filmmaking history, but his start was anything but remarkable. He had to master the art of learning from mistakes. Today, Spielberg is the standard most filmmakers hold themselves up to. Steven Spielberg didn't start from making blockbusters such as Jurassic Park, E.T and Jaws; he started with mistakes but didn't give up on movie making. Today, he is renowned for producing some of the best movies ever to grace television screens in almost every home.

Spielberg was rejected by the University of California several times, but he was a failure who mastered the act of seeing setbacks as challenges in disguise. He didn't allow that rejection to define his life. When one of his earliest ventures 'Laugh o gram' studios went bankrupt because he was unable to run that business successfully, not only was he hounded by his creditors, people lost confidence in him. Yet, Steven didn't learn failure. Instead, he learned how not to bankrupt a business.

Let us look at the life of another man. Today, many years after his death, Disney studio remains the brain behind top-grossing movies such as "Lion King," "frozen" "Snow White" and "Mickey Mouse." However, Walt Disney was fired from a newspaper because he was "uncreative," but that never dampened his spirit. Thrice, his startups failed. Once, his producer stole his character. When he decided to start the Mickey Mouse character, his friends advised him against it. However, Walt had learned lessons few people learn in life. It didn't matter to him if Mickey Mouse failed. Such was his outlook that it is safe to assume he would have gone on until he found the perfect character.

You should imbibe the same spirit. See defeat as a learning curve, and look at failure as a springboard which is necessary to propel you to unexplored vistas. Learn to see failure the way Jobs and Spielberg saw it as a call to do more.

You don't have to be defeated, learn from others

"Life is all about evolution. What looks like a mistake to others has been a milestone in my life. We are humans, and we make mistakes, but learning from them is what makes the difference."

- Amisha Patel

If you are waiting for defeat, the kind that was experienced by Abraham Lincoln, J.K. Rowling, Napoleon and many others in history and contemporary times, you may wait for so long that it becomes too long. Their path is different from yours, the business or the projects they were involved in are different from yours, but there is one thing you can relate to; life evolves, and so must you. By learning from the mistakes of other people, you can preempt setbacks and take proactive steps.

If you are reading this book to become a better business leader, you must take the next statements with all seriousness.

If you are in business or engaged in any of life's endeavor, you must always remember that "you do not have to fail to learn." You do not have to learn from your defeat if you can learn from other people's mistakes.

Like Amisha Patel, you can make the mistakes of others a teaching experience for you. You can learn from their experiences even if you never had the chance to meet them. You can perfect their errors and avoid their mistakes.

There is a reason why this book is filled with many examples; I desire that these examples contained here should serve as guides for you to prevent you from making these mistakes.

If you cannot learn from Abraham Lincoln's persistence, then you should learn from J.K Rowling's ability to maintain her coolness and knock on the next door. If you cannot learn from Thomas Edison's ability to be objective and dynamic enough to try different methods to get one result, then you should learn from the failures of the people closest to you. They have tales to tell about the victories they have won after years of disappointments and defeats.

Read historical materials, engage with successful individuals in, and outside your field. Their words will not only shape your decisions, but their counsel will also give you direction. One thing of importance to note is that nothing is happening to you that hasn't happened before. Study history and learn how people managed to wriggle out of such tight corners.

There is a reason why books are filled with so many examples. It is because of you. It is because of any individual who is willing to learn from people's mistakes. Don't stop at reading; apply what you read. Don't stop at listening; apply what you have heard and read. Don't stop at applying; move on to mastering, and continue to evolve.

In conclusion, defeats will always come, but you don't have to fail if you can learn from others. Setbacks will happen, but you do not have to be thrown back by what happens to you. Learn from each defeat, get back on your feet, spin things around, get started once again, and never forget the lesson you have learned.

YOU ARE YOUR BUSINESS

CHAPTER FOUR

WHY YOU NEED TO BE CURIOUS AS A LEADER

"Curiosity is the fuel for discovery, inquiry, and learning."

-Anonymous

The importance of curiosity

Millions of years ago, the earth as we know it was filled with gases. These gases came together and formed an aquatic environment, which made aquatic life possible. However, aquatic life existed solely for a while until some aquatic beings ventured to the land, partly out of curiosity and partly due to necessity.

Perhaps, they were propelled by the curiosity to experience what existed beyond their immediate environment. As they stayed on land, they began to develop features that could support life on land and water. These animals were called amphibians. Their fins began to change to claws, their gills began to form into lungs, and their extremely permeable body surfaces covered by soft scales changed into semi-permeable body surfaces with tough scales.

Curiosity also led these amphibians to seek for newer experiences as they sought for life that existed on trees. This got them beaks for cracking strong nuts and seeds, and feathers for moving from one location to another and claws for digging up worms and defending themselves. Soon, they were basically birds.

This continued curiosity propelled both aquatic and terrestrial life forms to produce the most intelligent and the most advanced form of animals, primates, with humans at the top of the chain.

Curiosity has not subsided with humans, rather it quadrupled. The world we live in today was built from mere formless gasses into a world of tech and gleaming skyscrapers because of the curiosity that man inherited from his ancestors. When ancient man only had stones, he turned those stones into hunting tools and fire-making devices. When the early man had only fruits to gather and had small prey to chase, he turned the forests into farmlands and domesticated the feral creatures to tame ones.

Man was curious, and he was driven by the instinctive and intrinsic desire to inquire, discover, and learn about his environment.

Curiosity led man to build industries from farms; curiosity led man to set up institutions of learning to pass on their knowledge and to set up a government that will distribute resources equitably. Curiosity made man build bridges to connect distant territories; curiosity made man build airplanes and ships to ferry him from land to land.

Curiosity made the early man ask questions about space. It made the early man ask about the denizens in space, about the living conditions outside earth. It was curiosity that took man to the moon and brought things from the moon back to earth. Curiosity is the reason why medicines were discovered, cars were invented, and technology continues to develop. If the world is more habitable today, it is because of man's curiosity.

This is not a book of history neither is it a book about science, but it is a book that contains information gleaned from science and combined with historical facts to present to the reader the importance of curiosity in leadership and other spheres of life. As a business person or as an individual with business interests, it is important to start with curiosity, continue with curiosity, and sustain your business with the attitude of curiosity.

Curiosity will make you ask questions; questions will lead you to new destinations; new destinations will lead you to new dimensions. As a businessman, it is going to be hard for you to achieve success while doing the same thing everyone is doing, the same way they are doing. To succeed, you must either learn to do new things or do old things in new ways.

Boredom arises from the absence of curiosity. Stagnancy comes from a lack of curiosity and retrogression springs up from a lack of curiosity. What would the world have been without the curious minds of its great leaders? What would nations have been without the curious minds of creators, inventors, innovators, and other creative thinkers who shape their destinies?

Without innovation, this book would have been written on countless pieces of parchments or enough scrolls to take up all the available space in your living room. Thanks to the curiosity of the inventors of modern printing press, you can now read with ease. Thanks to smartphones and the internet, you can now keep a library in your pocket.

In the words of Robin Sharma, "if you want to succeed in business or stand out as a leader, you must have boundless curiosity and an open mind." Curiosity is extremely important; curiosity is extremely vital; as a matter of fact, curiosity is one of the most important characteristics any leader should possess.

It opens up new markets; your product will sell better if it is developed from a process that started with creativity, is fueled by innovation, and is delivered with efficiency. You have to ensure that you and your business are forever at the top of the curiosity game, asking questions, and devising products and services to answer the questions.

How to develop curiosity

"Curiosity is one of the most valuable characteristics one can possess. When coupled with fearlessness and determination, that's freedom."

-Anonymous

Albert Einstein remains one of the most talented, intelligent personalities to ever walk this earth. His work and thoughts are responsible for sweeping changes in education, religion, invention, and other aspects of human existence. What does he credit as his greatest skill? Einstein says, "he had no talent whatsoever but a curious mind."

If Einstein had reported himself as talented, it would have made the discoveries associated with him seem like an exclusive preserve; something nobody else can attain. If his answer had been that he underwent years of serious and torturous training, this would have excluded everyone but a few who can endure such training. But because his answer was curiosity, it means we all can be curious, we all can be like Einstein. You can be like him too.

Followers need a curious mind, but most importantly, leaders need the kind of passionately curious mind that Einstein had. Without this kind of curious mind, your vision will be shallow, your solutions too feeble to stand alone. People will lose confidence in you as a leader, opportunities to make a difference will be missed, and change will sweep you away.

There are several ways to develop and sharpen your curiosity irrespective of your personality, background, and your position within an organization.

We all can develop a curious mind if we follow the following steps.

- **Adopting a beginner's mindset:** Most leaders grow up too early. Most leaders get strung on the idea that being responsible and work-oriented means being serious and remaining stuck in a repetitive pattern. Not only does this mindset of theirs affect their creativity, but it also set them at a disadvantaged point where they are less receptive to ideas from the "younger generation."
As a leader, however, it is pertinent to know that to develop curiosity, one has to adopt a beginner's

mindset. A beginner's mindset is one that is open to new ideas, and isn't cluttered and shuttered by theories and ideas that are outdated. A beginner's mind is open to exploration; it is open to questions. It is only with a beginner's mind that curiosity and creativity can be developed.

- **Be constantly inquisitive:** to be truly curious as an individual, and as a leader, one must be very inquisitive. What this means is that one must constantly be on the lookout for something new, something different, and in some cases, it might mean consciously asking questions about the old. This was the secret of Einstein and other great minds. Every scientific theory was borne from a place of 'inquisition.' These inquiries or (questions) lead to possible hypotheses; the hypotheses lead to experimentation and experimentation leads to a theory. This same path of inquisition can be followed by a leader. Leaders should ask others for their opinions and perspectives on different matters. Who knows what discoveries lie at the end of your inquisition? It is the literal way of digging for gold.

- **Be observant:** As a leader, you should never underestimate the power of noticing and perceiving things quickly. When it comes to leadership, every single detail count. The problem with most leaders is that they live either in the past or they are lost in the future. While these may have advantages, it makes them less aware, hence less curious. If you notice nothing, then you will ask about nothing. As a leader, to develop your curiosity, you need to be more into your environment, be more into people and of course, learn to pay keen attention at all times.

- **Be the leader that tries something new always:** there is nothing new to be discovered if you are stuck to the same old routine(s). There are no new discoveries if you are marooned on the same island of thoughts. If you want to develop your curious mind, be the leader that is always willing and ready to try something new. Trying something new will expose your mind to new points of view. Do something different, adopt "unfamiliar" methods. Find ways to change your style without altering your principles, and you will indeed achieve more.

Curiosity represents the engine and moving force for achievements. So, get yourself a healthy dose of it, or you will be stuck in a spot for far too long.

How to inspire curiosity in others as a leader

Being curious as a leader is good but not good enough. Being a curious leader without curious associates or curious followers could be frustrating as well. Being curious might be a valuable tool which can be used to steer the ship forward, but without inspiring curiosity in others, the ship will not sail smoothly.

Having a team that comes up with ideas gladdens the heart of a wise leader, and the legacy every great leader hopes to leave behind is to see their followers become as they are; curious, creative and in control.

Here are few tested and trusted ways to inspire curiosity in others.

- **Learn to lead by example**: Every leader must know that people will listen to what he says, but people will do what they see their leader do. There is almost no way to inspire curiosity in your followers if you are not curious yourself. Curiosity isn't a new management fad that can be picked up and practiced. It is a skill that must be practiced, perfected, and transferred. A leader that asks questions will naturally have followers that ask questions. A leader that is a keen observer will automatically have followers who are also keen observers. To inspire curiosity in others, be curious first.
- **Pair your team effectively:** the strength of a leader is not known entirely from the things he can do alone. The strength of a leader is known from how he can effectively manage people. In every organization or business, you will find different

categories of people, the conservatives and the liberals, the introverted and the extroverted, the reserved and the outgoing. It is common knowledge that every conservative individual will love tasks that keep them indoors while the extroverts will love the outdoorsy tasks. As a leader, pair the introverted with the extroverted so they can explore new challenges. New challenges always have a way of inspiring creativity in individuals.

- **Give your team members tasks, not assignments**: there is a big difference between tasks and assignments. An assignment is what an individual is capable of doing because it is within their capacity. Carrying out assignments increases the chance of getting bored and reduces the possibility of being curious. Tasks, on the other hand, are assignments which may be way beyond the scope of the individual. Tasks demand that the individual steps out of their comfort zones, do something different, or do things they are not familiar with. To effectively inspire curiosity as a leader, assign more tasks than assignments. You will be glad you did.
- **Reward Curiosity:** Every leader must learn to reward curiosity even in its simplest form. Single out the individual that paid more attention to detail or did something different. Celebrate a team that showed ingenuity and curiosity because nothing inspires as much as rewards. A reward system not only encourages curiosity; it inspires curiosity and

creative thinking in the whole team. When people have something to look up to, they are more inspired to do more.

Curiosity is a staple for successful leaders; they live it and breathe it. Even better though, you should try to inculcate it in your team.

YOU ARE YOUR BUSINESS

CHAPTER FIVE

LEARNING TO LOOK FOR THE MOST IMPORTANT ELEMENT/QUESTION
The devil is in the detail

"The difference between something good and something great is attention to detail."

- Charles R Swindoll.

Many lives have been ruined, and businesses run aground because important elements or details were ignored when they were discovered. One of the strongest skills a manager should have, and (if missing) develop is the ability to spot essential details.

Leadership involves a lot of work. It involves being curious, as we have learned from the last chapter; it involves self-belief, as we have seen in preceding chapters. It involves looking at the big picture all the time, but most importantly, it involves a bit of critique as we look at the small picture.

"Details" is one word every leader must pay attention to. Details can be understood by looking at every situation as a whole situation made from a combination of smaller parts.

For example, a car might seem like a single piece of machinery, but on the flip side, a car is a machine made from the combination of different parts. Different parts make up the interior; different parts make up the exterior, and various components smake up the engine. The advantage of looking at a car as different parts combined to make a whole is that it becomes easy to 'fix' any faulty part.

The same illustration holds true for a business or an organization. There are different departments that make up an organization, and various individuals that make up these departments or units. What this means is that without a detailed leader looking keenly at the organization *in units*, a lot of things will go wrong from just looking at the big picture alone.

There are several important elements that are critical in a business environment. They may range from tangible to intangible, and can be physical and non-physical entities. Physical or visible elements which are important for a leader to look out for include the structure of the business space, the uniqueness of the product and the product's packaging.

Non-tangible details every leader should pay attention to include the efficiency of service rendered or provided, the efficacy of product or service, the response rate of the company to complaints and queries, effective feedback and detailed documentation.

It must be noted that the difference between good and great is in 'if' and 'how' attention is paid to both the visible and invisible factors. Businesses that fumble, companies that crumble and leaders that stumble are the ones who pay less attention to these essential details.

Businesses that blossom and thrive are the ones that pay more attention to the essentials because we live in a world where a lot happens all the time. You could have the best product ever, but if you have not paid attention to scout what the market needs, for instance, you have left out a detail. That detail will render your awesome product useless and unmarketable.

Leaders are often confronted with activities all competing for priority. The consequence of this is that important things get done and whatever is classified as unimportant is left unattended to. While this may sound convenient, one thing managers or leaders need to know is that if they don't care to look out for the critical elements, why should other people do?

Check out the following reasons why paying attention to details is extremely important.

If a business or a leader doesn't pay attention to details, he/they are seen as

- **Disorganized**: have you ever bought a product that was poorly packaged or have you ever ordered for a service which took forever to be delivered or was poorly delivered? If you have, your confidence in such product or such service delivery likely dropped. The ineffectiveness is the result of a few details that were not properly monitored. As a leader, it is important to know that public perception is all-important and once a product, brand or business is perceived as disorganized, it is almost impossible to change that perception
- **Not credible enough**: Fortune 500 companies are ranked in such elite class and are trusted by their end-user, customers, and clients because of credibility. Credibility is the result of many things but most

importantly, the ability to pay attention to detail. If a business does not look out for the important elements that their customers love and remember them for, they will lose credibility. All businesses are built from trust, and all relationships are erected and sustained on a foundation of trustworthiness. It is the little details that form the big picture of credibility.

- **Makes you susceptible to being conned**: this point is important for individuals who are new to the business. If your co-workers, staff or associate know you have a knack for not looking at the finer points, then you will become vulnerable to attack as they will comfortably perpetrate acts like fraud and act irresponsibly by turning in poorly-done tasks. A business that handles their matters casually will also be susceptible to individuals like amateur hackers and identity thieves. While it must be stated that every business is susceptible to attacks, the more detailed businesses easily detect the attacks and build fortifications against such attacks while the less-detailed are more exposed and less disposed to fortifying themselves. As a manager or a business leader, do not ever forget the words of a famous speaker, trainer and business owner, Chris Denny who said: "Attention to detail is not about perfection, it is about excellence."

What other goal is there to strive for in business other than excellence?

If you are critical, be constructive
All great leaders know that accomplishments are the cumulative effects of critically reviewing your present until the present becomes better than the past, and the future becomes better than them all. In John Foster Dulles words, "a man's accomplishment in life is the cumulative effect of his attention to detail."

Successful leaders in business and other spheres of life understand that the moment you get satisfied with statuesque, that is the moment you begin to decline. This is why they examine everything "critically "until they get the results they are looking for.

To this end, every business leader has to explore the concept of positive critique. It means you have a keen eye for details and you are dissatisfied with mediocrity. Positive critique is often aimed at a process and not the person, which is what makes it different from being a critic. Critics, most especially destructive critics, always target the individual and their abilities with an emphasis on their failures, disabilities, and frailties. In the end, such criticism leads to loss of esteem, trust, and in extreme cases, the leader or business may lose the input of the person permanently.

On the other hand, when you are critical of a process, it allows the individual at the receiving end to know that there is a better way of doing what was done — it means that there are higher standards that can be aspired for. The rewards may not be immediate, but they are certainly rewarding. Every leader should have it at the back of their minds that they can correct the process so long as they are constructive in their criticism. The idea is not to destroy the individual but to eliminate all forms of mediocrity in the individual.

The best part is that you don't have to be the only one who is detail-oriented, your associates can be too, if only you will inspire them to be. Read on to find out how.

Ways to inspire a culture of critical observation in the workplace

"If you place emphasis on getting little things right and address everyday problems that come up, you can encourage the culture of attention to detail."

– Richard Branson

Apple, Virgin, Adidas; this is what these companies had in common that allowed them to rise up the ranks. They have absolutely brilliant products and extremely detailed leaders that were sometimes accused of being too critical.

Truth be told, if you pay attention to detail, you might develop an attitude of being critical about everything — every single detail. The story was told of how Steve Jobs was obsessed with detail, shapes, and the entire outlook of his products. This obsession with detail made *Apple* products highly sought-after until today.

The advantages of being critical are beyond overwhelming; it is, however, extremely stressful for the manager or the head to be the only 'critic' in the business or organization. Leaders are responsible for inspiring that attribute in others so that just the way companies like *Apple* and *Virgin* that have now become companies known for their detail even after the exit of their owners, the business can also be known as a business that is detail-oriented.

Here are a few steps a leader or a manager can follow to inspire a critical but positive mindset in the workplace.

- **Zero tolerance for Mediocrity:** The buck rests on the table of the leader if the business progresses or retrogresses. Any leader looking to lead a business that is very detail-oriented has to have a zero-tolerance for mediocrity. Little but continuous acts of being highly critical of avoidable errors and flaws can and will lead to a culture of excellence. A healthy culture is everything. Once a leader can establish a culture that frowns at the wrong things but smiles at the right things, such a leader can be called a success. This can only be successful if the leader is positively critical, to begin with. Once replication of a zero-tolerance for mediocrity has been established, a culture of perfection has been formed.

- **Build the culture around an ideology**: It is important to build your team around an ideology. Not only does this encourage team spirit, but it also helps to spread the positive culture, especially when new staff members are employed or when new personnel visit. "This is how things are done here" is a familiar phrase that is commonly used in most establishments. What this represents is that the business or establishment has its ethics founded on an ideology. Ideologies always ensure that people have a rallying point.

- **Reward positive "critique";** Any form of reward from the leader goes a long way, which is why leaders should use the tool of reward or creating an effective reward system to ensure that attention to detail/positive critique is rewarded. The leader can employ and deploy any means to ensure the reward is given. You could give gifts or create an award for the best individual or departments for the month.

- **Punish when necessary**: this point is very related to the point on having zero-tolerance for non-detail-oriented output, but it is important still. One of the best ways a leader can encourage attention to detail is by punishing defaulters when necessary. A leader should set in place penalties that remind the team that only excellence in all ramifications will be accepted.

Any leader that follows this list religiously will eventually discover that not only have they inspired positive critique; they have also enshrined the culture in their business.

CHAPTER SIX

USE SUCCESS TO FIND SUCCESS

The aim of going into business is to succeed. The success might come in different shades and forms – it could be achieving the vision of the business, turning a profit, or achieving a goal. Whatever the case, an entrepreneur can usually tell when they have achieved success in their business venture. The business journey of an entrepreneur is typically rife with difficulties, challenges, setbacks, and disappointments. It's a thorny path of hurdles that entrepreneurs must take in their bid to achieve what their heart desires. Little wonder why business success is so appreciated and celebrated by business owners.

However, there have been reports of businesses failing after achieving success. They suddenly go bankrupt or record a sharp decline in performance that ultimately leads to their failure. A major anomaly that is common to these failed businesses is the failure of their owners to build on the successes that have been attained. The owners of these businesses failed to capitalize on their successes and expand their enterprises. And they paid heavy prices for their mismanagement.

True success in business is not something you can attain quickly; your business needs to be successful over a long stretch of time for it to be considered a total success. One of the worst things that can happen to your business is if it stalls after recording its first major success, going no further and simply losing significance over time. While it is possible to use your competencies to achieve short term success in business, it becomes increasingly difficult to depend on only your capabilities to make your business successful in the long term. You would need more than just your competencies to keep your successful business afloat.

To start with, for your business to be able to achieve and maintain success, it needs to be built on the foundations of a big idea and a strong vision. The business idea tells you the problem you are trying to solve and what you have to do to solve it, and the vision gives you an idea of where you want your business to be in the near and distant future. If you don't have a vision for your business, then you are not in a position to determine how successful your business would be in the long run.

For instance, if you don't know where you expect your business to be in 10 years, then you wouldn't have the clarity to make the decisions that would keep your business successful over that stretch of time. Apart from having a big business idea and a strong vision, here are some other points that will help you dredge your success and keep your business successful.

- **Make customer service a vital part of your business's philosophy;** Many consumers have canceled an intended purchase or service acquisition due to poor customer service. You probably have canceled your plans to buy something at a shop in the past because of the way the shopkeeper treated you, or the way the overall service delivery stank at the shop. When this happens, it impacts negatively on sales and can damage a business's reputation. Turn up your customer service game, because doing so will lead directly to making more sales. Remember, loyal customers are easier to sell to than one-off buyers.

- **Build on your marketing;** Effective advertisement is directly proportional to sales, given that other factors are in your favor. Large corporations spend staggering amounts of money on marketing their products because they know that they would make that money back, with profit, on the results of their marketing efforts. However, you don't have to break the bank trying to market your products. There are many inexpensive marketing schemes you can use to your business's benefit. An age-old way of marketing is by word of mouth. Spread the word about your products among your peers and encourage them to do the same. Soon, you'd have garnered a host of new ready-to-buy customers. For this to happen, though, you need to consistently provide good customer service delivery, leading us back to the first point. Apart from using word of mouth, you could also market your products by using promotion kits, handing out promotions with your invoices, promoting your business on the pages of local newspapers, offering free seminars or workshops, and creating effective partnerships with companies that offer complementary services.

- **Use the internet to your advantage;** Many people do research of products they want to buy online before going to purchase them at a store. With evolving information technology, it has become incredibly easy to create a website. You should leverage the reach of the internet to showcase your products and services to a seemingly unlimited number of consumers. Depending on your type of business, you could also use social media to showcase your products.

- **Cut down on business costs;** Although this appears to be a no-brainer, it is an uphill task to tackle. Business costs eat into your finances like termites eat wood. The more you can cut down on unnecessary expenses, the higher your returns will be. A first step towards cutting costs is tracking your expenses. You need to know exactly how much you're spending to know how much you can save. Fortunately, there are many online and mobile platforms out there that can help you track your expenses effectively. They also make the entire process less strenuous and more time effective.

- **You must find and keep the best employees;** Employees are the moving forces of your business. They are the wheels that enable your business to glide from point A to point B. If those wheels are deflated, your business will find it difficult to make progress. Find the best talents you can afford, and be sure to treat them well so that they will stay loyal to you and your company's objectives and vision. If you fail to keep your employees, you'll inevitably end up spending time and money recruiting new hands now and then. This is not an ingredient for making success.

Every business is going to experience some form of success; only a smart business leader knows how to ensure that success doesn't run out.

CHAPTER SEVEN

CREATE AND BE IMAGINATIVE

"Logic will get you from A to B. Imagination will take you everywhere."

-Albert Einstein

It was Adon Davids who said, "if you fail to evolve with time, you will dissolve in time." The message contained in this quote isn't just for business leaders alone; it is for every emerging leader. Many leaders have failed to evolve, and they have become jetsam and flotsam floating aimlessly in the ocean of life. Evolution is a constant process, but only Creativity and imagination are the constant variables.

Times and seasons will come and pass, but what will differentiate two leaders or two businesses from each other is the presence of creativity in one and the absence of creativity in the another. A 'creative leader' is always ahead of their time, and this makes them leaders of a progressive revolution, innovators of new ideas and creators of products or services that have never been witnessed.

No matter how logical you are; you are limited without an imaginative mind. This is because, with an imaginative mind, there is no limit to what can be done and what length can be covered. Those who herald industrial revolutions are those with the powers of creativity and imagination.

Computers were once large, clunky and ridiculously expensive until *IBM* stormed the computer hardware scene. By being creative, they were able to bring freshness and difference to personal computers. Sadly, computers were still expensive and not easy to use, especially for non –technical users. Despite the technological intervention of *IBM*, sales continued to drop, the demand from users continued to wane, and something needed to be done urgently. The computer industry needed a break from the norm and a deviation from convention.

It was at this moment in history that two Steves arose, Steve Wozniak and Steve Jobs, who brought creativity and ingenuity to the computer industry in the form of Apple computers. Not only did they revolutionize how computers looked, but they also revolutionized how they worked and how people used them. Today nearly 2 billion people use or have used the extremely sleek and sophisticated Apple products, from personal computers to tablets and the iPod.

Depending on where you live, either in the boisterous and extremely metropolitan city of New York in America or the bustling and bubbling city of Lagos in western Africa, taxis are a part of cosmopolitan traffic. Taxis are cool when compared to other forms of public transportation and also afford the privacy that is missing in commercial buses or metro buses. However, they were expensive to use, hard to order, and could be unsafe at times.

Well, that was until March 2009, when what today has become the largest and fastest-spreading taxi-hailing company in the world, *Uber*, introduced an entirely new module in the use of Taxis.

Today, Uber services are available in sixty-seven countries across various continents. The founders spotted a gap and filled it so creatively that the rest of us had to carve out a large of the transport industry and hand it to them as a reward for ingenious creativity and innovation. Spurred by Uber, other taxi companies like Lyft, Hailo, Grab taxi, and Gett have all tried to capitalize on the success of this American company. Uber continues to hold the larger share of the business as a prize for being the first to break new grounds. Until the day one of the other companies spots a new creative question, and answers it with its services, Uber can remain safe in the knowledge that they control this particular market.

Let us look at another common example. For many years, researchers, historians, and lovers of knowledge had to pore over pages of encyclopedias or use updated versions of online encyclopedias to get research materials for their research projects. Not only was this time-consuming and energy-sapping, but the information also was often not sufficient enough. Then came the emergence of Google, the world's largest search engine online. Today with the swipe of a screen, you can find just about anything, even if you are not a researcher. Google spotted a creative gap and eased into it. It soon became so firmly entrenched that it is almost impossible to imagine what life would like without Google.

This is the beauty of creativity; it is a very critical quality lacking in most businesses; hence, the collapse of most businesses. The internet was a product of imagination and creativity; our cell phones are a result of creativity and imagination. Think of social network platforms that occupy our time and our lives today, and you will understand how valuable creativity is.

Dear reader, creativity, and imagination can do more than improve the standard of living; it can also save lives. Take the example of Alexander Fleming, whose creativity and ingenuity saved millions of people from the early 19th century to the present day because of his discovery of penicillin, a strong antibiotic.

Without creativity, you will not stand out. When your business does not stand out, you are only one disaster away from being wiped off.

How to be creative as a leader

"The simple process of focusing on things that are normally taken for granted is a powerful source of creativity."

-Edward de Bono

Do not believe the old wives' tale that has been peddled about creativity. For many years, creativity has been limited and restricted to the artistically inclined such as writers, painters, sculptors, and the likes. While that is part of the truth, it is not the entire truth in itself. In today's very competitive world, leaders in every industry are now expected to be creative in order to distinguish themselves from the competition.

Creativity and imagination work together, and both need to be employed by a leader to create results that will be both outstanding and extraordinary. Every leader needs a dose of imagination to be creative the same way they also need creativity to lead effectively. Use the tips below to boost your creativity index.

- **Start from where you are**: there is no such thing as the right time for Creativity. If you want to lead effectively, if you want to move your business from the ground floor to the top of the food chain, you have to start being creative immediately. The only limit to being creative are self-imposed limits, which could be a result of your decisions, conditions, and conditioning. As a leader, you cannot afford to delay or dither. You must begin as soon as possible, or else your dreams will remain dreams. When dreams remain dreams for far too long, they become permanent dreams, unable to come to life.

- **Break away from convention**: The biggest enemies of creativity and imagination are convention, conformity, and repetition. Most leaders are stuck to the same patterns and mode of doing things which make them stereotyped and cogs in the wheels of change. As a leader, you must do away with statements that shoo away creativity. Such statements may be good in ensuring a routine culture is maintained; however, it is terrible for creativity. Creativity says there is more than one way of doing things; creativity says old patterns, old thoughts, and old ideologies are to be dumped or refined. Creativity says success can be yours

- **Be curious**: a curious individual will always stumble on something new; an invention, a discovery, or an old technique that needs a little refinement. The curious man never runs out of creative ideas. To be a creative individual, you must learn to be curious about information; you must learn to be curious during conversations and on every occasion. Curiosity is responsible for most of the inventions, creations, and innovations which are currently making the world a better place to live and work. Once a leader loses his curiosity, he loses his ability to make amazing discoveries.

- **Be intentional about creativity**: there is so much power in intention. When a leader adds intention to creativity, there is so much they will do differently. Remember whatever you ingest, you will digest, and whatever you digest, you will eventually reflect in your work and in your life. Creativity requires intention. Visit museums, art galleries, do a lot of travel, and try poetry. To be more creative, you have to read a lot, listen to music of different genres, engage in activities that are way out of your comfort zone, and dabble in arts. Going out of your way to acquire knowledge will make you more receptive to new ideas when they pop up.

- **Try disruption sometimes:** Doing the same thing all the time will only result in the same results. This is the issue with most leaders, but there is a solution to this. Try to be disruptive in whatever you do. Change your thought pattern. Alter your work pattern a little bit. If you stay away from crowds a lot, try mingling more. If you mingle a lot, experiment with solitude. Being disruptive can involve you adopting daydreaming and exaggeration if you are naturally conservative. By breaking your pattern, you can stir your creative juices and develop the powers of your imagination.

- **Get inspired by nature**: the idea behind the invention of the airplane was inspired by the sight of birds in flight. The submarine was inspired by large mammals and fishes like whales and sharks. Many more products and devices we make use of today were inspired by nature. If you are observant enough, there is so much inspiration out there for the individual who pays enough attention.

- **Don't forget to ask questions** and unleash the inner child within you if you want to be creative. Creativity is much more than a series of actions. It is a lifestyle which if followed by a leader, will guarantee success.

How to promote creativity in the workplace?

"A good teacher can inspire hope, ignite the imagination, and instill a love of learning."

-Brad Henry.

Every good leader is usually a great teacher, and they always desire to see their followers become as they are and even much more than they are. As a leader, you should be able to ignite the imagination of your followers not by how creative you are, but by allowing them to explore their creative potentials. By doing this, innovative thinking will not just stop at the top but will spread from the top to the bottom of the business or organization.

- **Let the teamwork in environments free of limits**: Studies have shown that the less conventional and structured environments or activities are, the more creative the individual will be. To promote creativity in your business, allow your team members to work without limits (psychological, environmental, and physical), unreasonable deadlines, limiting office wear, and unexciting work environments. This doesn't mean there won't be boundaries or timeframe for work to be turned in or a sense of order in the workplace.

- **Have a diverse team**: most leaders only work with individuals that have similar personalities and abilities as theirs. While this has its advantages, it has its disadvantages also. To promote creativity in your business, ensure you build a team made up of diverse personalities with each having different skills and capabilities. Team members with different strengths will inspire others and spread creativity across.

- **Let the team know that failure and experimentation are encouraged**: As a leader, you must understand that an atmosphere that doesn't encourage failing, discourages creativity. It is the responsibility of the leader to get team players to understand that failure is not a taboo, and experimentation is allowed. Interestingly no experiment ever fails; there are always so many lessons to be learned, provided the team has the right mindset.

- **Avoid "but"**: when you use the word "but," it imposes limits and restrictions on the minds of the team members. It tells them there is next to no space for creative ingenuity. A mind that is limited and restricted is a mind that will be inhibited from tapping its creativity. Leaders must ensure that the team members are opened up to this failure-free method of attacking tasks.

- **Tell them "what" and not "how"**: it is the responsibility of every leader to tell the team members what should be done clearly and directly. Telling the team exactly how to achieve the goal without allowing them to try it out destroys creativity. This will take away the team's ability to solve problems their way.

If your plan for your business is to offer the same products and services as your competitors, then the chances are you are always going to have to play catch-up. That is not too easy or healthy for you, especially if you are still a small business. Instead, carve out a creative solution and make yourself get noticed. Allow creativity to flow your team, and sooner rather than later, your business will strike a gold mine.

CHAPTER EIGHT

BUILD A TEAM THAT UNDERSTANDS YOU

"Great things in business are never done by one person; they're done by a team of people."

– Steve Jobs

What is a team?

You may have been confusing a group with a team. They may look alike, but they do not function in the same way. They might work together in a room, but groups are hardly in one accord. Groups work as an independent unit with each member trying to outshine the other, but a team works as a unit, with each member working in consonance with the other and all working together to achieve one goal. With groups, a business may survive, but with a team, a business will thrive.

For clarity sake, a team is a group of individuals of an indeterminate number who are all bonded together by a common cause and who all work together for a common goal. A group, on the other hand, is a collection of individuals also of an indeterminate number who work together, but not necessarily with the same personal goals.

As a leader, you should be aware that there are different kinds of teams found in all kinds of business or organizations. All of these teams have their roles; most importantly, all of them have their differences and similarities, check them out and see which best fits your leadership style.

- **Team by function:** this is the most common type of team that can be found in a business. The role of this team is self-explanatory from the name; a functional team is a team that is related by the function they play.

- **The disparate Team by function** (cross): this team is also known as a cross-functional team. In this team, the individuals mostly experts, all come together from different departments and with specialties to work on a project. A cross-functional team can be assembled by the leadership for a high-level project or task.

- **The organized, self-directed team**: this is a kind of team that makes the leadership excited. A self-directed team is not put together by the leadership or management. A self-directed team is a team made up of proactive members of an organization who come together of their accord to achieve a goal or to ensure a project is completed.

- **A Virtual team**: This is another common example of a team because of the technological advancement in the business industry in today's business world. A virtual team may not be in one location, but they all play their respective functions. Virtual teams can be made up of individuals that speak different languages, have a different job description and stay in different countries, and they may have little to no physical contact but are all working towards one goal with the aid of technology.

As a leader or manager, it is important to know each team, so you can know how to work with them and use them to achieve your goal.

The Advantages of a strong team

"Individually, we are one drop. Together, we are an ocean."

– Ryunosuke Satoro

No matter how skilled an individual is, no matter how effective they work and no matter how fast they deliver on their timelines, no single individual is stronger and better than a team. As the Japanese poet, Satoro, said, "As an individual, the person is as strong as a drop, but together, a team is as powerful as the ocean."

Yes, it might take considerable time, training and effort to get all members of a team to top speed and top shape but individuals will certainly achieve more and cover more, working in association with a team. There are so many advantages to working as a team. Let us check some out.

- **Working as a team saves time and energy**: even a little child knows that an extra hand makes any task easier. When you work as a team, tasks are completed faster, stress is reduced, and energy is saved for other pressing matters. As a matter of fact, describe your T.E.A.M as a group TESwhere *"Together, Everyone Achieves More"* with little effort.

- **Working as a team allows for synergy**: synergy occurs when the sum of different parts is greater than the parts. To better understand this, check out an orchestra. A harmonious orchestra is a result of different musical instruments in sync. For example, no matter how fast a production team works, they need the distribution or logistics team to get their products to the end-users. Their results can only be commensurate to their efforts if other team members work with them.

- **Working as a team inspires peace and unity in the workplace**: when individuals work in seclusion, there is a tendency for competition rather than complementary efforts. Unhealthy competition is the greatest threat to peace and unity, which is why most leaders always advocate that individuals work as a team. In a team, people's strengths complement the weaknesses of others, ideas are exchanged, and a healthy working environment is fostered and maintained.

- **Working as a team improves efficiency and productivity:** teamwork increases efficiency generally and aids productivity irrespective of the scope or nature of the work.

- **Teamwork eliminates unnecessary hierarchy**: sometimes, certain roles in an organization occupy positions and play very little to no function (especially the hierarchal positions). With effective teamwork, the unnecessary hierarchal structure is dissolved and converted into useful and functional roles. This allows for even distribution of tasks.

- **Teamwork provides one of the best avenues to learn**: sometimes companies and leaders do not have the time or opportunity to transfer knowledge or train their staff except on special events like retreats or special company training sessions. As a leader, why not take advantage of pairing individuals to teams: pair stronger skillsets with weaker ones, pair the old with the new and pair the amateur with the professional. Then, sit back and watch learning and training occur.

Qualities to look out for in a team that understands you

"Find a group of people who challenge and inspire you, spend a lot of time with them, and it will change your life."

–Amy Poehler

You may have a fantastic idea, product or business. You may have worked on it solo for years, and suddenly you are ready to take the next step – finding and selecting your team. It is at this point many entrepreneurs and businessmen fail woefully. Most people find it hard to build a team that understands their specific requirements.

However, building the right team is easy if you can follow the below-listed rules.

- **Choose the individual that best fits the role**: Ensure that the candidate's skill, background, and pedigree match the requirements you want before you include them in your team. This might seem easy on paper, but it is difficult when it comes to implementation. You might need the help of a trained Human resource individual to help with this if you are not a good judge of character. Nevertheless, never compromise on this. Putting an individual in a role that they cannot perfectly play is akin to putting square pegs in round holes. You will eventually be rewarded by mediocrity and disappointment if you make a choice based on sentiments.

- **Communication is key**: Except you are hiring a cleaner that will clean up after everyone has exited the building, you should ensure that whoever you are adding into your elite team should be able to speak coherently, write clearly and understand whatever is said.

- **If they are organized and disciplined, pick them**: a team is meant to work together in pleasure and under pressure. If you must select team members, you must look out for team members that are disciplined enough to meet deadlines, self-controlled to work on their emotions, and organized enough to ensure assignments and tasks are detailed and always on point. These major qualities are very important, and you must have a very keen eye to notice these details on the first day of meeting an individual.

- **Look out for proactive and resourceful individuals:** You would not want team members that bring efforts to you rather than results. You wouldn't want a team member that loves excuses or one that loves been told what to do; nobody does too. So, when looking for a team that understands you, look for individuals that are proactive enough to do more than they are told to do and are still resourceful enough to get the job done at all cost.

- **Look out for team members with the right character:** you would not want a skillful but arrogant member on your team. You would not want a rabble-rouser and a disloyal member of staff on your team. This is why no matter how well-dressed or suave an individual is, ensure that they have the right character. Look for traits such as honesty, loyalty, team spirit and optimism, and the right attitude to work in team members.

It is only teamwork that makes the dream work. Therefore, nothing is as critical as picking the right 'men' for the job. If you want your business to prosper, pick a team that understands you.

How to be a team player as a leader

"It is amazing what you can accomplish if you do not care who gets the credit."

– Harry Truman

Most leaders today want all the credit for themselves. Some leaders allow their team to take the flak for failure, but they take the shine for victory or in moments of victory. These sorts of leaders are not leaders, but rulers. This sort of leaders are not team players but team destroyers.

Leadership is much more about team playing than leading. Leadership involves the daily process of inspiring, motivating, interacting, guiding, and working with the team in some cases as one unit.

You can be a team player and an effective leader; here is how.

- **Be always on hand to help but do not hinder**

Every leader that is a team player should always be on hand to help. Team members will always have questions to ask, team members will always have suggestions, and it is almost certain that they will head to the leader. Here is where it gets tricky; a great leader solves these issues by teaching "how to" and not doing the tasks for the team members. The purpose of helping them is to assist and not to restrict the team member from playing their role effectively.

- **You must know your team**: knowing the team might not be a challenge when the business is still small and in its formative stage. However, as the business expands, the team members also increase. This is, however, no excuse for a leader. It is important for every leader to know most of their team members, notwithstanding.

- **Always ask for input** and feedback; Most times leaders are caught up in a "cul de sac," and they seem to do all the work themselves, without asking for input or considering inputs from team members who could be colleagues or subordinates. Asking for input even if you wouldn't put it to use makes the team members feel like a unit and makes them have a sense of belonging.

Take these words of advice; the best leaders are always great at team play.

CHAPTER 9

GRATITUDE, A LEADER'S BEST FRIEND

"People will rarely work at their maximum potential under criticism, but honest appreciation brings out their best."

— *Dale Carnegie*

Workers may work harder when they are condemned for their last performance but have you, as a leader, ever wondered about the result of being spurred to work by a reassuring pat on the back, an uplifting handshake and a hearty well-done?

Gratitude has many definitions and can find many applications in different situations, but in this book, it will be defined as a quality of being thankful before, during, and after an act/service has been rendered. Nothing keeps staff members in a company's employ like thankfulness and gratitude. Nothing is more responsible for staff retention, as the act of taking out time to recognize and celebrate the efforts and results of staff.

Studies have shown that not only does this develop the individuals' ability, but it also makes them work at their maximum potential. There are many reasons why gratitude is important in the workplace. Let me highlight some of them here.

- **Gratitude inspires loyalty**: Leaders must understand that almost every worker wants to change their jobs, but no one wants to leave a family where they are appreciated. Gratitude is one of the most important ways to show team members or workers in a business that they are much more than tools used in achieving a goal in a transactional relationship, where all they get is payment for their services. Loyalty cannot be bought. It can and must be earned, and one of the easiest ways to earn it is by showing genuine appreciation genuinely.
- **Gratitude encourages empathy in the workplace**: A workplace without empathy is a disaster zone waiting to happen. When workers do not feel that their efforts count, when they do not feel that they are noticed, they also act the same way towards their fellow colleagues and the management. In a workplace without empathy, you will find

individuals who are intelligent but lacking in emotional intelligence; hence, they lack the ability to feel people's pain. Lay down a marker by responding to the needs of your workers as humanely as possible.

- **Appreciated workers are happy workers**: have you ever walked into a business environment and gotten assailed on all sides by grumpy faces and fierce looks? If you haven't, then you must be one of the lucky few who haven't, because workplaces like this actually exist. One of the reasons that could contribute to unhappy working conditions is a work environment where workers don't feel appreciated. Leaders must know this: appreciated workers are always happy workers, unappreciated workers are often unhappy ones. When a leader takes out time to tell the worker s how grateful they are in words and action, the reward of such is always a brighter and a better working environment that promotes productivity.

- **Gratitude and appreciation allow workers to form bonds with the company**: many companies have suffered from brain drain because they failed to appreciate the effort and the results of their best hands and best minds. Paying bonuses and salaries are not sufficient enough, and do not hold a candle to genuine appreciation for a job well done. If you master the art of appreciating your workers, they will stick around longer, irrespective of other offers they may be getting. Gratitude will earn you loyal and diehard workers, and save you the cost of hiring and training a new worker.

I need you to know that it is important to know that the best is always locked up in people and it takes a leader who appreciates the little that has been done to bring out the best in the worker.

How can you appreciate your team in the workplace?

There are many ways to show appreciation to deserving workers. From kind words to gifts, the list is endless, but we can just check out the following.

- **Kind words always work**: every leader should know how to apply the tool of words and kind gestures. Some leaders, however, forget to deploy this tool. While most workers understand that it is mandatory to receive their wages, they also subconsciously expect a pat on the back from the boss or a hearty well-done from the management.

- **Sending personal messages**: there are many ways to show appreciation to workers in any business or organization. Leaders who want to send a message that is both personal and professional can send text messages, appreciation cards, or even emails to the worker they intend to appreciate. Such messages create a personal touch; they tell the worker that you respect them as a person as much as a team member.
- **Special recognition:** there is a reason why most businesses or organizations choose special days, weeks, or months to identify, celebrate, and appreciate workers with outstanding service or performance. It is because it has a dual effect of recognizing and encouraging other workers to follow the footsteps of singled-out individuals.
- **Special lunch or dinner**: Leaders can organize special (or even surprise) lunch or dinner outreaches for appreciation and gratitude purposes. Formal or informal, it creates a family feeling within your organization and creates a camaraderie that can translate into renewed synergy.
- **Awards at company events**: You can organize end-of-the-year award ceremonies, quarterly award ceremonies, etc., to appreciate and show gratitude to

workers. These events can be very helpful in fostering team spirit and loosening up your employees.

- **Gifts and special reward systems**: Little tokens to appreciate stand-out embers of staff are always a catch. Other reward systems may include paid vacations, scholarship for kids, business training, and, paid seminars.
- **Use group meetings and newsletters**: this method is cost-effective and very effective. As a leader, you should learn to use the occasion of daily, weekly, or quarterly milestones to appreciate staff generally. The use of newsletters or business magazines to appreciate the contribution of workers works quite well as everyone likes seeing their name in print.

- **Have a wall of fame**: the wall of fame exists in most companies, and you can use them for appreciating workers that have put in extraordinary work and service to the company.

How to promote the appreciation culture in your workplace

Every good and commendable act should be a culture that pervades the work environment. As a leader, you need to promote a culture of appreciation and gratitude within your work environment. Here are a few steps to help you along.

- **Let your appreciation be sincere:** gratitude without genuine emotion is an activity in futility. Not only will people see through the façade, but the recipients will also feel slighted. As a leader, your gratitude should be true, direct, and personal. Appreciation shouldn't always be generalized, and every appreciation should be backed up with a message or a lesson for the listening audience. Avoid grandiloquent speeches and unnecessary stories that leave the recipient red-faced. Also, make that show of gratitude as soon as possible. If the action you're appreciating happened at the beginning of the week, don't wait till the end of the month to appreciate. Do it as soon as possible.

- **Ensure that the attitude of gratitude becomes a culture:** if appreciation comes only from you, it might be effectual, but what is more effective is when a culture of appreciation spreads from top to bottom and from bottom to top. The direct manager/supervisor can appreciate the good deed; the team members should also appreciate the individual. If all of this is done, harmony and team spirit are increased, and a spirit of healthy jostling gets instilled in the workforce, which is perfect for maximizing efficient service delivery.

- **Celebrate progress and results:** the phrase "only results matter" has done more damage than good to the work environment. While it must be emphasized that results are to be desired, one tested and trusted way to get best results from individuals is to celebrate the smaller milestones too. They build up to become the progress you want to see. learn to praise workers for being proactive, resourceful, and showing initiative. Do not wait for the results to manifest, appreciate the thought process too.

- **Praise in public and criticize behind closed doors:** it is expected that every worker should be confident enough and have strong self-esteem, but this is not always the case. As a leader, it is important to know how to administer the tools of condemnation in moderation. Praise people in public, but do not make pointed criticism in public. It introduces some damage to the self-confidence of the subject of the criticism. It leaves them on the defensive and makes it less likely that they will appreciate the point you are making. Instead, point out errors in as private a situation as possible. You can still pass the message in public without making pointed barbs at the subject in question.

- **Appreciation should be evenly distributed**: there are always overachievers or top shots in teams, but some team members can also be underperformers. As a leader, this might be a very slippery road to tread. While you must highlight the performance and outstanding role played by individuals, you must also ensure that the appreciation is evenly distributed so that the whole team feels appreciated and no-one is left out.
- **Start from top to bottom:** gratitude is not for team members alone. It is also for team leaders. Learn to appreciate the divisional heads under you. Do not gloss over their efforts, and move straight to the team members. Start by appreciating team leaders, departmental heads and move down the rung. Make sure everyone gets a bit of the praise.
- **No act is too little to be appreciated:** big wins or small wins, great victories or narrow scrapes, all represent wins for you. They are

all entitled to be celebrated, appreciated, and memorialized. This might seem like a time-wasting or cost-intensive gesture, but it doesn't have to be. Sometimes, a simple appreciation speech at the end of routine meetings for efforts made during the week is enough. A round of applause or a handshake may even suffice. They all elicit the same psychological response in the recipients.

If there is any place that gratitude needs to be cemented as an attribute worthy of emulation, it is your business and workplace. Gratitude is the soul of continued and renewed commitment. It builds a healthy work environment where every member is striving to achieve beyond their potentials.

CHAPTER TEN

HOW TO TREAT TEAM MEMBERS

Many leaders, managers, directors, and business owners alike believe customers are the only ones that matter to their business endeavors; after all, they are the reason that the businesses exist in the first place. However, this notion is far from the truth. In fact, your team members are as important as your customers, because they are in charge of rendering services to your customers, and the satisfaction or dissatisfaction of your customers depend directly on the mental and physical state of your team members.

Therefore, keeping your team members happy is as vital for the survival and success of your business as treating your customers well. Treating your team members well does not only entail raising their wages, although that is an undeniable step in the right direction. It also entails communicating with them better, showing sensitivity and awareness to their plights and circumstances, motivating them, creating and implementing beneficial workplace policies, encouraging and sponsoring employee training, and incorporating good employment perks or benefits.

Big companies like Marriott and Google offer certain benefits to their employees to help motivate them and make them feel great at work. At Google, for instance, employees are allowed to bring their pets to work, they are given free healthy meals at work, offered months of paid maternity and paternity leaves, and so much more. Marriott offers hotel services at discounts to its employees. Employees who have worked at the company for up to 25 years get to stay for free at any of the company's hotels worldwide.

Marriott and Google are large corporations and can afford to offer these services without securing any losses, but that is not to say that small and medium-sized companies cannot offer employee benefits, even if they would be to a much lesser degree. Monetary benefits are good and desired by all, but sometimes those inexpensive smiles, courteousness, respect, and kind gestures can go a long way towards making your team members feel at home in the workplace.

Why you should keep your team-members happy
It is important for team members to feel good at work because of the multitudes of ways their positive emotions can influence their performance and productivity. When team members are certain that the company cares about them, they are encouraged to give more to the company. They work harder for the company and are more passionate about the work that they do. Apart from an obvious increase in productivity, treating team members well can bring about more benefits. These benefits include:

- **Improved customer service and customer relationships:** Customers are very observant of the situations of things at a company. They are quick to notice if a company's employees are happy or sad at work, according to the service they get from the workers. When employees are happy, they are more willing to attend to customers well, and therefore their relationships with the customers get stronger.

- **Less stress and fewer sick days;** A happy team member has less work-related emotional baggage to deal with, and this translates directly to feeling less stress. A team member who feels less stress would call in sick less often than one who shoulders a behemoth of stress.

- **Lower turnover rates;** It's a no-brainer that dissatisfied team members don't stay at a workplace for long. They tend to look for greener pastures elsewhere, leaving you scrambling for people to fill the vacant positions. Making fresh recruitments can be quite tasking and expensive. On the contrary, when team members are treated right, they feel at home and are therefore less willing to leave the company. This means that you get to save more, as you don't have to spend time and money trying to recruit people to fill vacant spaces. Furthermore, when you reward hardworking employees with promotions, others would be more likely to stick around and work. Also, there are certain employees who can prove difficult, even impossible to replace, because of their expertise and talent. You don't want to lose such employees to other companies or worse; you could lose them to a direct competitor!

- **Attraction of talent;** When people know how well you treat your employees; they will be attracted to your company. It's not a coincidence that employees are drawn to certain companies, such as *Google*, *Facebook*, and *Marriott*, as they have learned of the ways these companies treat their employees and the way they expect to be treated if they are employed. When you employ exceptional individuals to work in your company, they, in turn, make your company even more attractive by using their massive talents to drive your company forward. It's a big positive cycle!

- **A cut down on litigation:** If you don't treat team members well, there is a risk of lawsuits being filed against your enterprise. Certain issues such as employee safety, benefits, and wages are important issues that have the potential to damage the reputation of your company and cost you money, if not properly managed. Thanks to social media and the tons of company review websites out there, it doesn't take much time nowadays for news to spread. Once your company has managed to secure a negative reputation in public, it would become increasingly difficult for you to recruit distinguished or talented employees.

The above-stated points are just five of the numerous benefits you can accrue from treating your team members well. These and other benefits reveal the reason why treating team members well is not a luxury or an option, but an absolute necessity, for a company that wants to succeed. Team members who are treated with respect, care, and dignity consistently put themselves in situations where they have to go the extra mile to serve the company. They feel they are part of the company, and therefore, treat it like their own.

How to treat team-members well
If you are not treating your team members well, you are inadvertently refusing to build a strong team of personalities that can make your company succeed in the short and long run. Here are some recommendations as to how to treat your team members:

- **Extend your help and assistance beyond the office and to their personal lives:** It is good to help your employees with office-related matters, but it is not recommended that you stop there. You must be observant and sensitive enough to know when a team member is going through a personal crisis and get into a conversation with them about the issues. For example, if a team member is finding it difficult to rent an apartment and the situation is becoming uncomfortable for them, stick a leg in and help them out in whatever way you can. You could speak with the manager of the apartment they want to rent, or, if you have the time, find out and recommend a similar apartment to the one they want. By doing so, you give them an impression that you are willing to do anything in your power to assist them; and this breeds a certain loyalty in them towards you.

- **Be humble enough to relate to them; don't act like you are above and beyond their reach:** No matter how tempting it might be, don't act in ways that make your team members think you feel you are superior to them. Do not condescend at all. Learn to get close enough to your team members to observe when things are not going well with them, and help them out by sharing your experiences and anecdotes with them. As a leader, your team members may likely place you on a high horse, but when you break that barrier and put yourself on their level, they become more liable to open up to you about their circumstances and their challenges.

- **Show support and care for your team member's personal life:** This is not to say that you should become creepy and stick your nose in matters that do not concern you, but from time to time try to show that you care about your team member's personal space. If you are celebrating at the office, allow team members to bring in their significant other, if that's what gives them support. Show your team members that they are more than just worker bees to you.

- **Tailor your approach towards your team members' personality:** Get yourself acquainted with your team members' strengths and weaknesses as regards their education, knowledge, skills, habits, and talents. When you want to designate certain duties to your employees, give them tasks that they naturally excel at performing, not one they are known to struggle at. Allow them some flexibility as regards how they want to solve certain problems or how they want to complete projects, as long as their methods are not opposed to the company's philosophies and professionalism. Create an avenue through which team members, senior or junior, can make recommendations concerning how the company should be run and how challenges should be tackled. If team members are stuck with a problem, suggest further training or assistance by senior team members to help them get ahead.

- **Empower and develop your team members to increase productivity:** You should have a working knowledge of the team members who are more ambitious and willing to take on more tasks and challenges and motivate them to do so by empowering them with the knowledge they need through training and supervision. Put them in a position to make their own decisions about certain matters without having to defer for higher authorities to act. When you train diligent employees to become better, you not only motivate them to perform better but also improve the company's productivity. Also, you must reward good work consistently. You could use markers such as customer service, sales, and completed projects to score each team member's overall performance and reward outstanding team members. You may set up an employee of the month award, for example, which could be a free meal, cash, or another sort of gift. You must create a level playing field and ensure that all team members have equal chances of performing and winning the award.

- **Make communication a necessity:** You must communicate with your team members often and respectfully. There are several modes of communication nowadays, with phone calls, emails, text messages, direct conversations, and even social media. Know what platform to use to convey specific messages, and be as respectful in your approach as you can be without sounding patronizing. By communicating with team members, you might get to know their strengths and weaknesses, their challenges and fears, and their support system. This information can prove valuable while making certain decisions in the company.

Furthermore, you must be conscious of your choice of words when communicating with a team member. Don't be flat or unconvincing; be intentional with your words. For example, instead of saying, "Here is the next project for you to work on," you could say, "You did a wonderful job with the project you undertook the other time. Because of your great attention to detail and expertise on the subject matter, we have decided to give you another project similar to the last one, as your work stands out sharply from the rest." Everybody likes to be appreciated and motivated. When you make your team members feel that they are irreplaceable and exceptional, they give more to whatever project they have to undertake.

- **Be a good listener:** You need to listen to your team members consciously and attentively. In your team member's voices, you can usually find ideas and insights that can take your company to greater heights. So do not make the mistake of listening for the sake of listening. Listen to your team members because you want to; because whatever they have to say deserves to be heard and has a place on the table. If your team members are not satisfied with the conditions at the workplace, you can usually pick up their frustration in their words and subtle actions. Similarly, you can also pick up positive feedbacks from conversations with your team members.

Every team member should be treated well at the workplace, as this makes them feel appreciated and make them more apt to give their all to their work. As a manager or business owner, you should not create an environment in which team members are afraid to speak up, feel insecure or cannot wait to get a better job elsewhere, because of your lackadaisical attitude towards their wellbeing. You must create an atmosphere that promotes peaceful coexistence, effective communication, and loyalty between yourself and your team members.

Dealing with difficult members of the team

However, there are times when you may be taken for granted and even taken advantage of. Sometimes in the workplace, you might be on the worse end of a team member – manager relationship, such as is the case when dealing with difficult team members. Difficult team members can be a menace at the workplace and can frustrate your efforts as well as those of other team members. They have a proclivity for pulling the team back and seem to enjoy doing so. If you don't know how to handle a difficult team member you might find yourself in a challenging situation with this kind of team members in your team. Apart from being sore, difficult team members can derail other team members and compromise their focus on their tasks. Additionally, they can:

- Refuse to contribute reasonably to certain objectives of the team that they don't agree with.

- Spread negativity across the team, thereby creating more difficult team members.

- Influence diligent and loyal team members to not give their best to the team project or objective and by so doing, reduce the overall productivity of the team.

- Break the chain of teamwork and poke a hole in the coordination in the team.

- Resort to abusive behaviors, encourage the use of unprofessional speech or action or instigate team members against one another.

- Impede the overall performance per unit time of the team.

- Inflate the costs and push the timelines of projects.

In light of all of these negative effects that difficult team members can have on the team, it is imperative, if not crucial, to know how to deal with them appropriately. Dealing with difficult team members can be quite tricky because you have to strike a balance between refraining from unprofessional actions or speech and using your command, power, or authority to handle the situation. When dealing with difficult team members, effective communication is your most important tool and your deadliest weapon.

As a first step in solving the crisis, you must understand that most of the time, difficult team members are what they are because of certain underlying factors. They may be under severe family stress, lack the motivation and inspiration to work, be ill-suited to their current role at work, need support from the boss, have reached the ceiling of their capabilities, or be unreceptive of negative feedback. In any of these underlying factors, you must resort to using communication as a way to fill in the gaps and get tour difficult team members back on track. Notwithstanding how large your team is, if one team member has a problem and decides to vent out his frustration on the team, the entire architecture of the team could collapse and fall apart. That's why it's important to nip the situation in the bud before it gets out of hand. Below are tips, in stages, that can help you deal with difficult team members.

- **You must be a good role model for your team members:** The way you interact with your team members, clients, and customers can impact the way your team members behave in the workplace. If your team members notice that you get away with unacceptable behavior, they are apt to practice the same. You can avoid inappropriate behavior in your team by shunning it yourself and setting a good example instead. You must practice self-control, integrity, empathy, and professionalism at the workplace to demonstrate to your team members that you expect them to exhibit the same behaviors.

- **You need to understand that there is a problem:** Usually, if there is a problem, it shows in the words and actions of the difficult team member. When you notice the problem, you need to accept it as a problem that needs solving. Do not panic or be afraid to confront the team member about the problem. As a leader, you must always be ready and willing to address issues between yourself and any of your team members or between your team members. By accepting that there is a problem that needs to be solved, you put yourself in a problem-solving mode and get yourself ready to take the necessary actions towards solving that problem.

- **Sit them down and communicate:** As mentioned earlier, you must be able to have an effective discussion with a difficult team member, as this is the most potent way of solving the problem. Make them feel comfortable in the conversation. Let them know that they can trust you with any problems they are facing and that you are willing to do all that you can to help them out. In case they are not aware of them yet, let them know of the behaviors they are exhibiting at the workplace that are detrimental to the quality and pace of work, as well as the morale of the entire team. This way, you get them to understand their role in the big picture and how they fit into it, and how a change in their attitude can help undergird the team's performance.

- **Proffer a solution to the problem at hand.** Once you have succeeded in gaining the confidence of the difficult team member, you can then put heads together to think of a solution to the problem. The proffered solution must both be able to effectively address the problem and be fair to yourself and the team member. Make them pledge to commit to changing their ways and sticking to the solution, and ensure that they state clearly that they agree to the tabled solution.

- **State your commitment to holding them accountable for their behaviors.** You must put it forward to the team member that they will be held accountable for their actions henceforth, and that there might be consequences for actions that are deemed opposed to the team's objectives and proper functioning.

Realistically, there is no one-solution-fits-all for problems regarding difficult team members. You must, as the leader of the team, help your difficult team members as and when necessary by proffering solutions that are considerate of their unique circumstances and challenges. Whatever the situation, these tips should help get you on track in your quest to treat your team members well:

- Use "we" instead of "I" when conversing with your team members. When you use "I," it creates an impression that what you're talking about is all about you, and not necessarily considering the interest of the team.

- Speak coherently and clearly and ask for clarifications when your team members say something you do not understand.

- Ask questions as a means of moving your team forward; for example, "What do you think would be needed to complete this project." And listen attentively for feedbacks.

- Replace "but" with "yes, and." According to Jennifer Oleniczak Brown of *The Engaging Educator*, "but" shuts down conversations and "yes, and" opens up discussions. For example, if one of your team members want a vacation and it's not possible to grant them one at the moment, instead of opening your statement with "but", you could say, "You want a vacation, and I sincerely don't think it's the right time for one, so let's discuss about it."

- Perfect the art of nonverbal communication and use it masterfully. The way you stand, sit, or look in a conversation says a lot about your state of mind, and it sends a message to the person with whom you're conversing. On the flip side, you can also pick up cues from a team member's speech if you watch their nonverbal gestures closely.

- Listen, think, and then speak. Any other order endangers the conversation and your relationship with team members.

- Hold team members accountable for their behaviors. Treat everyone in your team fairly and equally; shun preferential treatment.

- Show your team members that it's alright to make mistakes. This boosts their creativity.

- Be mindful of the words you use. Use the acronym W.A.I.T (Why Am I Talking?) as the lens through which you filter your speech. Know when to listen and when to talk, and always choose the best words to convey your message, while remaining utterly respectful and humble.

Your team is as strong as its members. Your members are as good as the way you treat them. Treat them right and well, and your business will grow. Make them feel like co-owners and partners, and they will work like co-owners.

YOU ARE YOUR BUSINESS

CHAPTER ELEVEN

LIVE IN THE PRESENT
A matter of perspective: failure and success

"Only those who dare to fail greatly can ever achieve greatly."

-Robert F. Kennedy

The phoenix was a beautiful, mythical, and legendary bird that was said to have lived in Arabia. Periodically, the phoenix gets burned to ashes. From the ashes of this old phoenix emerges a younger, stronger, and faster phoenix. Till today, the phoenix is celebrated as a creature worthy of emulation.

There are lessons every leader can learn from the rebirth of a phoenix. Failure is never permanent, even if the situation seems and feels completely overwhelming. Success cannot be measured by the absence of failure. Sometimes, failure is one of the steps in the build-up to outstanding success.

If you judge the destruction of a phoenix as being negative, you would be right. If you look upon the resurrection instead and declare the event positive, you would also be right. The only constant is that after its destruction, the phoenix emerges a new bird, ready to take on the world again. Success and failure are not situations; they are perspectives.

The thought of failure as a fear-inducing, tear-inducing, shame-inducing event is held by most people. They dread failure and keep it uppermost in their minds. Interestingly, the more individuals try to avoid failure, the more they seem to be attracted to failure. Focus on success instead of failure.

Without failure, Thomas Edison wouldn't have discovered over nine-thousand ways by which the incandescent light bulb couldn't be made. Those nine thousand ways helped him discover the one perfect way. Without failure, the Wright brothers (Orville and Wilbur) wouldn't have found a way to design the airplane.

The words of one of the greatest leaders that ever lived, Robert. F. Kennedy captures it all when he said: "Only those who dare to fail greatly can ever achieve greatly." Failure is simply a matter of perspective; just the way success is. What you make of either of them is what they will become for you.

Moving beyond the past
For many leaders, success becomes an illusion because they have gotten caught in an all-familiar trap: the trap of remembering the past rather than learning from it. Truthfully, it is hard to suppress memories, especially if they are unpleasant and filled with regrets, wishes, and defeats. However, it is not a wise idea to allow what happened in the past stop you from doing the best you can in the present.

When talking about the past, it is also important to state that it is not just past failure that can hold you down. Sometimes, even past success can put you at too much ease and allow complacency to creep in. When that happens, you get hooked on the past and fail to advance.

By holding onto the past too tightly, you can turn a blessing into a curse. Like Oscar Hammling once opined, "The greatest enemy of present happiness is past happiness too well remembered." To help you live more in the present, consider the following tips.

- **Decide to forget the past**: Highs or lows, success or failures, so long as they are in the past, they should be left where they belong.

Pick lessons from them, and move into the present already.

- **Never blame others**: One of the keys to continued success is stopping the blame game. Continually blaming a person or a system will never change the situation. Blaming others will make you bitter and stuck in the past rather than make you better and ready for the future.

- **Learn from the experience**: one of the best ways a business leader or an individual can forget the past (its bliss and burdens) is to learn from it. If you made a poor business choice, don't regret it; learn from it. If you made a wrong call, don't fret about it. You should learn from it instead. That is the best thing to do.

As a leader, there is more to build on in the present and much more to achieve in the future if you know how to learn from your past experiences.

How to use the experiences of the past

"All my successes have been built on my failures."

-Benjamin Disraeli

Benjamin Disraeli, the first earl of Beaconsfield, and former prime minister of the United Kingdom, definitely knows one or two things about succeeding as a leader. He has this to say about his failures;

"All my successes," he said "have been built on failures." Most people spend their time regretting the past instead of living in their present. If you are guilty of this, borrow a leaf from the words of author Karen Newman, who said, "it is important not to regret the past. Instead, you must appreciate all of your past experiences and find a way to learn from the negative ones."

The events of your past occurred for a reason. Some of them are bound to be self-induced, while others are a result of factors beyond your control. I do not need you to find out whose fault it is. I want you to realize that the past is the past, and there's little you can do about it. To maximize your usage of experiences you have acquired in the past, follow the steps below.

- **Understand what happened**: everything has a reason why it occurred. Every question has an answer, and every problem has a solution. Successful leaders know this, which is why rather than make hasty judgments and conclusions, they seek for clarity. Clarity means understanding the genesis of mistakes that happened in the past. Ask yourself personal questions, ask your teammates involved, and understand the error you made. If you do not gain clarity, you will find it hard to gain closure and move on.

- **Start using positive lessons**: lessons are meant to be learned for a reason. The lessons of your past are there for you not to repeat the same mistakes. If you fail to heed the lessons, get prepared to go through the same painful process that characterized your past mistakes.

- **Change your habits**: if you look closely at your past, you will notice that some of your failures were a result of your carelessness or high-handedness. If you identify any such bad habits, then you must seek to get rid of them and develop new ones in place.

Success is a combination of failure and success

"Make new mistakes. Make glorious, amazing mistakes. Make mistakes nobody's ever made before."

-Neil Gaiman

Success is a formula, and all formulas are made up of different constituents. Earlier in the chapter, we found out that success can be built on the foundation of failures, and how you can profit from your past experiences. We will build on that background now. On your path to success in business, it is essential to know that you will need the vital combination that success and failure represent.

Every single invention today was either a product of coincidence or pure trial-and-error experiments that had more than a fair share of setbacks and failures. This is the secret of most inventors, creators, and innovators. They embrace failure as a necessary part of their ascent into the history books.

Use failure as a drive for success

A lot of people suffer from a condition known as Atychiphobia. This condition affects as much as 90 percent of people in the world. Atychiphobia is known as a morbid fear of failure, which occurs when people let fear stop them from moving forward, achieving goals, and becoming successful.

Other people suffer from a condition characterized by fantasies about past successes and delusions of grandeur. As a leader, none of this is favorable for success. Rather, you should use your failure as further fuel to motivate yourself to succeed the next time. Here a few tips to help you with that.

- **Don't avoid challenges;** instead, confront challenges. One of the effects of failures is that it makes individuals avoid challenges and difficulties. Those who fail consistently are frozen by fear, held back by indecision, and grounded by the thoughts of the past. To achieve success, learn to confront your fears and challenges. Challenges are your chance to prove that you are worthy of the success you want.

- **Realize that your past success can be your greatest enemy**: when you realize that the greatest enemy of your present is previous success, You can use the lessons learned, the resources earned, and the opportunities gained as a stepping stone for better opportunities. Keep the success as a relic though, and it will keep you firmly in history.

- **Avoid complacency**: failure can cause complacency but success can also cause complacency. Complacency always results in mediocrity. You may have made a big profit, or won yourself lots of accolades; you may not recover fast from your last success, and you may be tempted to sit back, relax and enjoy the past successes or present success. This sort of complacency is the reason why most businesses fail, and most leaders stumble, so it must be avoided at all cost.

Failure has many definitions. It can mean everything except "Stop." Failing does not stop you from trying again. Succeeding does not mean you should switch on the backburners. Both of them are calls for you to try better. It is hard to repeat the success you have achieved; do not dwell on it so much that you acquire reluctance.

In whatever state your business is right now, do not forget Winston Churchill's words about failure and success. He said, "Success is not final, failure is not fatal: it is the courage to continue that counts." Do not get tied by the past; deal in the present.

YOU ARE YOUR BUSINESS

CHAPTER 12

MONEY IS A BONUS, NOT THE TARGET

"To be successful, allow your business look towards creating value rather than profit. Values lasts longer than profits"

Anonymous

It is true that every business venture aims to make more money than it is spending. In other words, it is the wish of every business owner to make a profit. This is an undeniable fact. However, it has been argued over the years by business experts that having a more grounded purpose for setting up a business is better overall for the business venture. For example, setting up a business to solve a certain problem while making money on the side gives the venture a stronger and clearer vision statement, one that resonates with the ideals of its workers.

Most of the big corporations of the world are set up this way – they are essentially created to help solve a problem, in the process of solving which, the company becomes profitable. An example of this sort of company is *Google*. The original developers of *Google* noticed that there was a vacuum in the field of search engines, as the existent search engines couldn't offer search results in order of their suitability to the queries. Thus, they created *Google* to provide a service that other search engines were not able to offer. Their goal was to occupy the gap that existed in the search engine world and create a world of their own where they would dominate. They have done just that – and have made quite a fortune in the process too!

Making money should not be the only target of an entrepreneur or business owner. When you leap onto the entrepreneurial bandwagon for the sole aim of making wealth, you may be severely fazed by the setbacks that are very often apt to show up. You may not be able to deal with poor situations when they arise in your entrepreneurial journey, because you never had a strong purpose for starting up the business in the first place. However, when you start a business with better ideals such as the freedom it gives, the chase, the intrigue, and the chase, you give yourself reasons to hang on when things are not going your way. Because of the vision you have for the business, it becomes difficult, if not outright impossible, for you to quit. The entrepreneurial venture becomes an itch on your skin that just won't go away; it becomes a calling, one that you can't NOT pursue. It becomes more than just a money-making endeavor.

When venturing into business, get yourself a mindset that preaches that "although success would be very much appreciated when it does come, its presence or absence would not be a determinant of the existence or non-existence of your business." You must hang on to the business even if success does not come in early. You must understand that entrepreneurship is a journey, not a day job or a get-rich-quick venture. The ultimate dream of every entrepreneur should be to disrupt the status quo in the marketplace and create an entirely new and different category of companies, which would bring the owner recognition, status, and wealth. These entrepreneurs venture into paths that have not been traveled in a bid to make a name for themselves and their companies, and they very often come out on the other side, victorious and rich.

A good example of this kind of entrepreneurs is the founder of *Facebook*, Mark Zuckerberg. He went into the social media space, disrupted it, and created a brand new, billion-dollar category into which many companies would later try to fit. We have discussed *Uber* before as another example of a disruptive endeavor that turned into a moneybag. *Uber* has created a brand, new category that was not in existence before it came, and following its daring endeavor came other ventures in the 'transportation network companies' category, such as *DoorDash*, *Sidecar*, and *Lyft*. The founders of these companies had clear visions of what they wanted to create and stayed true to their vision until it became a reality. To these entrepreneurs, money was only a bonus, not the target.

Another thing you must be wary of is becoming attached to a business venture, so much that it becomes exceedingly difficult for you to make objective decisions about the running of the business. You must view every business venture as a step in your journey, not your final destination. Having this mindset enables you to loosen up and be more objective when handling matters concerning the enterprise. If you come across setbacks that force you to terminate your business, don't be too bitter about it. Take whatever you have learned in the business and apply that knowledge to your future business endeavors. Do not view business as the first and last thing you'll ever do.

Although you can control certain factors and work towards achieving set goals in business, very often the outcomes or results that you get are not congruent with the efforts you put in. Therefore, while you set goals and work towards achieving them, bear in mind that you may end up getting results you didn't bargain for. When this does happen, make contingency plans to help you get past the ugly situation and forge ahead. Be optimistic about your goals, but also be realistic enough to know that things may not always go your way.

The ancient Greek athlete, Milo, developed strength and resistance by lifting a calf every day as it gradually grew into a cow. You can glean knowledge from Milo's tale by allowing yourself to grow stronger and better in your entrepreneurial journey. But this can only be the case if you view entrepreneurship as not a money-making venture but as a journey driven by your passion and spirit.

If you have this your mindset, you will notice that you are less weighed down by the inevitable hassles and downsides of entrepreneurship. As time goes on. you also become better at decision making, possess clearer insights, make better analysis, get better interpersonal skills, and make more sales. If you feel you can't go through the journey alone, you have an option of gleaning from coaches.

Some of the most renowned entrepreneurs in the world today have at a time in their entrepreneurial journeys had coaches from whom they learned.

Some of these entrepreneurs still had coaches even after attaining great success. That speaks volumes about the importance of holding someone's hand as you go through your entrepreneurial journey. As the founder of *LinkedIn*, Reid Hoffman says, "highly successful individuals live in a state of perpetual growth and development; they never stop learning, are constantly evolving and iterating, are always learning new things and exposing themselves to new challenges and adventures, and are not scared to use opportunities as they arrive." This kind of individuals pay more attention to the journey than any monetary rewards their business venture could bring them.

When you are too focused on the financial gains that may accrue from your business, you would be liable to miss out on vital learning opportunities in your journey. So, relax and take whatever comes your way in your stride and in goodwill. Learn from mistakes and missteps, improve and build on successes, and develop yourself into a truly exceptional entrepreneur.

In the world of entrepreneurship, the main goal should not be to make a profit but to create value, to change people's perceptions, to change the way they behave, or to challenge and change the way they live. This and this alone should be the purpose or aim of any entrepreneurial endeavor from the beginning up until the very end, if there is an end. It is true that while creating value, an enterprise might become a business when it begins to create wealth; at this point, the entrepreneur can modify the purpose of the venture to account for its monetization. But, at this point and all points in the entrepreneurial journey, an entrepreneur must have the sole aim of creating value at the forefront of their entrepreneurial ambitions.

Quite frankly, if you go into a setting up a business for the singular aim of making money, then you are not very different from an employee. After all, an employee goes to work from nine to five to earn money and make ends meet. In other words, leaving your job for a profit-driven business would have made no difference, apart from the increased working hours and more significant risks. You would be doing yourself a great disservice by pursuing entrepreneurship to make money – employment is a much easier alternative to making money .

So, if you have made up your mind to become an entrepreneur and a business leader, you might as well have the right goal in mind. And the right goal is not to make money.

CHAPTER THIRTEEN

INTEGRITY AND HONESTY AS ESSENTIAL COMMODITIES IN THE BUSINESS SPACE

""Integrity is telling myself the truth. And honesty is telling the truth to other people."

— Spencer Johnson

As an entrepreneur, you need honesty and integrity. As a person, you need honesty and integrity too. Most importantly, every business leader needs honesty and integrity on his resume, no matter the size of his organization or the reputation they have developed over the years.

Honesty is the innate quality of being honest, upright, noble, and upstanding while integrity is a track record of trustworthiness. It is the quality of being upright in thoughts, words, and actions. Your words are as good as your track-record of integrity and honesty.

Author and speaker, Spencer Johnson describes it in this way; "Integrity is telling myself the truth and honesty is telling the truth to other people" in business environments where customers need to be enticed. Truly, products need to be hyped, and marketability is the name of the game. However, there is still a place for telling the truth as a leader and a business owner.

The business place is an ecosystem made up of a leader, the workforce, the end-users or consumers, and the rest of the public. All these disparate parts are all connected as parts of one body, and function as one. As the leader, you are responsible for guiding the people around you and giving them their operational instructions. A single trace of dishonesty spreads like cancer, damaging your structure from inside out.

Why leaders need honesty and integrity
Many years ago, the commodity of trade in the market place was products, today the commodities of trade are people (i.e., human resources). Years ago, the pride of companies was superior products; today, most companies have outstanding products,

and the real difference is in customer relations and a strong business culture.

In the past, shadowy businesses could succeed by cutting corners, inflated figures, and blurring the lines. Today, to survive, you need wholesome practices. It doesn't matter how you do it; if you cheat your way to the top, you will be found out and punished. To make matters worse, a single incident can end a multimillion-dollar enterprise. It takes very little to get found out, and dealt with.

Therefore, as you lead your business from the front, remember that you are responsible for what your business does. You have to ensure that you are operating within the rules of your industry. There is no excuse for ignorance.

Since the turn of the century, we have been treated to examples of what happens to businesses that have been found guilty of failing the integrity test. Each time, this happens, the leaders cannot escape scrutiny. They get dragged in the mud whether they knew about the deceit or not. This is because the general belief is that it went on, under their directions, instructions, or passive support.

The consequence of the actions or inactions of these leaders end up costing the leaders their jobs, loss of share capital, loss of reputation, and a loss of valuable clients or customers.

Once you get tainted, you do not get a second chance ever. It is like a mirror with a crack; it cannot be whole again. I tell you today that every single one of your problems can be solved, and every mistake can be forgiven, except for those that deal with integrity and trust.

You get to deal with a lot of trust contracts as a leader. You have the trust of your investors; your clients come to you because they trust in you and your organization, and your staff members work in the belief that you are trustworthy. Damaging or breaking any of these contracts renders all the rest void, especially in the mind of the concerned parties.

As Williams Shakespeare said, "no legacy is as rich as honesty. If it was true then, it remains valid till now. Do you want a great and lasting legacy? Ensure you conduct your business with honesty and integrity.

Stories of trust gone sour
When he went on the Oprah show in the 2013 and made a stunning confession about how he had doped his way to victories, the sporting world

shook. For many years, Neil Armstrong had been the darling of the media, a maverick in the biking world and a cancer survivor. He was able to merge sport and business, which earned him numerous endorsements and a brand that was as strong as top business brands.

When the bubble burst though, the cycling world stood still, and his followers were left hanging by a thread. It was a shock and a stunning revelation. Just like that, he lost not just his title as one of the best-ever in the game, but also the trust of all his fans. Away went endorsement deals, and the brand he tirelessly built for years. Immediately, suspicions began to trail his name anywhere it was mentioned. His achievements were eroded, and a century from now, he will be recognized as a cheat first, before he is remembered as a cycling champion. He wasn't the only one, either.

In the early nineties and the early 2000s, Marion Jones was the darling of athletics and the queen of the sprints, winning race after race she participated in. She attracted the best of global brands, and the money, medals, and endorsements poured in. She was held up as a prime example of what pure talent, dedication, and discipline can bring to everyone...and then, suddenly, everything came crashing down.

Test results proved she had been cheating, and there was no way around that fact, even as she repeatedly denied. Banned and stripped of all her titles including her Olympic medals, Marion Jones faded into history as ye another who cheated.

This chapter isn't dedicated to exposing sports stars alone. Let us look at another more conventional case in the business world. In 2010, *Enron* was living the dream as a strong company; everyone wanted to belong and get associated with *Enron*. With over 20,000 staff members and over billions in revenues, the sky seemed to be the limit. By the end of the year though, *Enron* had filed for bankruptcy. How did this happen?

A lack of integrity in the accounting and the top management hierarchy sent the cards crumbling and crumble it did. *Enron* isn't alone in this cadre. When *Kmart* went bankrupt for the second time, every eye turned towards the management, and rightly so.

Bernie Madoff may be the biggest name in Ponzi history, but even his reputation wanes in comparison to Charles Ponzi whose name became synonymous to fraud. Charles, an Italian Immigrant, ran a pyramid scheme involving over 40,000 investors and costing millions of dollars. The result is that he became popular for the wrong reasons.

These are just examples of people who had to trade their success, influence, and position for a place in history's black books. These are just a few of the many brands who have failed the integrity game. Most brands never recover from that fatal mistake.

As a leader, you must understand one thing about honesty. It is no longer an option; it is now a necessity. The world is always watching and checking you for honesty and consistency. There is just no way you will escape with dishonesty.

If you are found wanting, it could be the end of your business and name in your niche,

How to inspire honesty in the workplace
You need everyone in your team to be honest as well. As a leader, honesty and integrity should be the watchword when you deal with your team, clients, and the public in general. Your team members are waiting for you to give them direction about the integrity level you are aiming for. Show them that dishonesty is welcome, and they will learn the game faster than you.

Find below a few options you can explore to inspire a culture of loyalty and integrity in your business.

- **Be an honest leader**: nothing sells honesty like honesty; every leader that desires to have honest workers must set the example themselves. As a leader, your word must match your actions. Your word has to be your bond. Honesty doe not come to everyone easily, but with an honest leader, even a difficult virtue can be imbibed with time.

As a leader or a member of the management, ensure that your promises are delivered on as promised. Take your promises serious and that culture will spread from top to bottom easily. A perfect leader commands and inspires integrity in all situations, even unpleasant ones.

- **Be tough on dishonesty**: Honesty and integrity should be part of the core ethics of any business. Not only does it make work easier, but it also creates an atmosphere of trust. However, honesty has long-lasting effects than just intraoffice purposes. This is why every leader should ensure that dishonesty in any member of the team, irrespective of role, be punished and held accountable for every act of dishonesty. Great leaders are tough on dishonesty, and if you want to grow your business to great heights, you have to learn to be tough on dishonesty and dishonest acts. Forgive everything but dishonesty.

- **Reward honesty**: when honesty is rewarded at every opportunity, you are sending a message that honesty is a required commodity in your environment. Acts of honesty should be noticed, applauded, and rewarded even much more than acts of talent and skill. As a leader, you can give out cash gifts; you can set up reward systems and special recognition programs. The intensity with which you frown at dishonesty should be mirrored in the way you reward base honesty and loyalty.

Will mistakes happen? Will lies be told? Will lines be blurred? Yes, but by instituting an environment where they cannot thrive, they will be discovered in time and get reduced to the barest minimum.

YOU ARE YOUR BUSINESS

CONCLUSION

In the scheme of things, no business is going to be exactly the same. You may be in the same market, offer similar products, allocate the same resources to marketing and yearn for the attention of the same clients, but your business will always have a different feel from every other one.

Clients who patronize two similar business will always come away with different experiences. Why is this so? Each business has a feeling, a spirit that clients can perceive when they walk in to do business with you. It is a sum of your products, the relationship between the staff members on the consumers' end, team-work behind the scenes, and the leadership you offer as the leader of the business. It is your sole responsibility to ensure that your business has a client-friendly, team-like feeling that encourages healthy competition, honesty, and creativity. They are the secrets behind business success.

Your business is going to look exactly the way you approach it. If you communicate straightforward commitment, and creative ingenuity, your business will shape up along those lines too. Your team members will key into your vision and join hands with you. Your clients will be able to feel the synergy and key into your vision. Add to this great client relationship, and there is absolutely no obstacle that can stop you from achieving success.

You may not exactly make the *Fortune 500* just yet, but allowing your business reflect your awesome personality will set you along that road faster than you ever imagined. In no time at all, you will make the journey from zero to hero in a flash. Your business is **your business, and no one else's.** Start leading today! Start leading now!

YOU ARE YOUR BUSINESS

YOU ARE YOUR BUSINESS

www.ingramcontent.com/pod-product-compliance
Lightning Source LLC
Chambersburg PA
CBHW060841220526
45466CB00003B/1188

www.ingramcontent.com/pod-product-compliance
Lightning Source LLC
Chambersburg PA
CBHW060841220526
45466CB00003B/1188